THIS DAY IN RECOVERY

THIS DAY IN RECOVERY

365 Meditations

Edited by Lane Campbell and
Katie Kandarian-Morris

Skinner House Books
BOSTON

skinnerhouse.org

Printed in the United States

Cover design by Rebecca McEwen
Text design by Jeff Miller
Lane Campbell photo by Yuriy Nutsa
Katie Kandarian-Morris photo by Jennaye Derge

print ISBN: 978-1-55896-863-9
eBook ISBN: 978-1-55896-864-6

6 5 4 3 2 1
25 24 23 22 21 20

Cataloging-in-Publication data on file with the Library of Congress

BEGINNING

Why We Decided to Write This Book

We, Lane and Katie, are Unitarian Universalist ministers who serve congregations. Both of us actively practice recovery in Alcoholics Anonymous, Overeaters Anonymous, and Adult Children of Alcoholics. And almost every week we hear cries for help from people seeking resources for folks struggling with addiction. In our pastoral relationships, mothers come into our offices looking for ways to get their child to stop doing drugs. Our colleagues need something to hand to congregants who are living with addiction in their families. People are battling addiction to food, to people, to alcohol, to drugs, to sex, to any number of other things. We see people desiring sobriety and having a difficult road getting there, who look to their faith to support them along this journey. We all need resources in these moments of our lives that seem too big to handle alone.

We decided to write this book because we need it for ourselves. We wanted to create a daily meditation guide that has as its source experiences with addiction. We wanted to create a resource, grounded in Unitarian Universalist values, that can speak to a broad range of theological perspectives. And we wanted to provide a way for folks to explore Twelve-Step recovery from a Unitarian Universalist perspective. This book exists so that we all may bring our hearts, minds, and spirits to this spiritually rich and profound experience of struggling with an addiction and finding recovery.

Each contributor to this book is a religious leader in Unitarian Universalism, a faith whose theology is expansive while holding on to the core values of freedom of belief, each person's right to seek truth and spiritual growth as they choose, and a deeper love that holds us all. We each hold a Unitarian Universalist perspective. And Unitarian Universalism is open to many interpretations of God, Higher Power, and trusting in something larger than ourselves. Though Twelve-Step recovery is founded in Christian values, much of its modern-day expression also embraces a freedom to choose what to place our trust and belief in. This book brings in perspectives of people who identify not only as Unitarian Universalist but also as Jewish, Buddhist, Christian, and more. Even if you are an atheist or agnostic in recovery or considering recovery, we hope you will find a home in it. These pages are founded in Unitarian Universalist beliefs and values but are ultimately for people who are spiritually seeking, for people who have an expansive view of the divine and even the not-so-divine.

This book invites us to engage in a short daily experience that will inspire spiritual reflection. Addiction is something we take one day at a time. This book is meant to bring us back to our spiritual center in those everyday moments when we are struggling, when we are celebrating, when we are not yet where we want to be, and when we are looking for inspiration, seeking to be of service to others and to our world. We want an extra tool in the recovery toolkit for those who are struggling with their own addiction, and we want a source of sustenance for those who are living with others engaged in that struggle. This meditation guide is meant to bring spiritual depth and inspiration to anyone, and especially to those living with addiction.

How to Use This Book

In the basic text of the original Twelve-Step program, written in 1939, a form is suggested for arising each day. On awakening we are advised to think about the day ahead, to reflect on our plans, and to allow whatever it is we consider the Ultimate to direct our thinking, so that we start the day fresh, in the care and direction of something larger than ourselves.

In order to adopt this healthy habit, it helps to have a guide for daily reflection, something that offers tools for daily sustenance. Many folks find their source of strength to be their relationships with other people. The Unitarian Universalist faith tradition draws on six Sources, of which the second is "words and deeds of prophetic people which challenge us to confront powers and structures of evil with justice, compassion, and the transforming power of love." This book offers a nugget of inspiration for each day of the year, connecting us with wisdom from a diverse range of prophetic people.

We find it helpful to set aside some quiet time for this reading and reflection. Even five minutes as you're having your morning coffee can be enough time to settle and prepare yourself for the day. Some folks may find that a deeper session of twenty to thirty minutes offers some of the same benefits as a meditation practice, such as lowering anxiety, enhancing self-awareness, and promoting emotional health.

Each chapter of this book is devoted to a Step and to a month, working through the year in order. You can begin by opening this book to today's date. Alternatively, if you are working on the Steps, you could begin with your current Step's month. If there are particular topics for which you are seeking some experience, strength, and hope, each chapter is also centered on one or two that match its Step.

Each day's entry offers a quote from a contemporary or historical source, some reflection inspired by that quote, and a question. The question can be used for meditation, for contemplation, or as a prompt for daily journaling.

Who This Book Is For

The fact that we are people with a strong spiritual background doesn't mean that we're unaffected by the struggles of daily life, our family history, and our layered life experiences. We need spiritually liberal tools to aid us. This book is an aid for people who are trying to get sober but are perhaps wary of some of the traditional daily manuals. It can also be a companion for people in long-term recovery who want something more focused on spiritual exploration or even on specifically Unitarian Universalist values. It can serve as a valuable resource for family and friends of folks who struggle with addiction.

This book holds a wide variety of perspectives, as it is our intention to hold spiritual space for a multitude of experiences in recovery. Its authors and contributors hold membership in Alcoholics Anonymous, Al-Anon, Adult Children of Alcoholics, Overeaters Anonymous, Refuge Recovery, and many other programs and have varying levels of experience in practicing these programs' principles. Each day brings an opportunity to hear a new perspective informed by different life experiences in recovery. We believe it is healthy for people in one program to hear experience, strength, and hope from folks in other programs. If you come across a reading that doesn't reflect your experience in recovery, try to listen to the wisdom of someone with a different viewpoint; if you find yourself resistant to their message, try to lean into your discomfort.

Recovery is both personal and collective. Some days' entries speak in "I" language, out of personal experience. Others are addressed to the collective experience and thus use "we." All of them embrace the both/and nature of recovery: something that is deeply personal to each individual while also being grounded in shared experience and in the truth that none of us can recover alone.

This book is not a substitute for a program of recovery, but rather a companion on your recovery journey. Or perhaps even an introduction to recovery.

It can also serve as an aid for Unitarian Universalists who want to engage in a regular spiritual practice and deepen their spiritual maturity. It is for any one of us who desires to live a more grounded life, filled with a sense of gratitude and serenity. If you are looking to deepen spiritually in your recovery, this book is for you.

OUR CONTRIBUTORS

The creation of this book has been a shared labor of love and a deep act of service. Without each of the voices reproduced here, it would not be available for people seeking recovery, or even just seeking the daily nourishment we hope it has to offer.

Each person named here has written a portion of this book, but no individual reflection is attributed to its author. We chose not to do so in order to respect the anonymity of the people who offered their voices in this book. And we wanted readers to be able to focus on each reflection rather than on a specific author. As the Twelfth Tradition of Twelve-Step recovery reminds us, "Anonymity is the spiritual foundation of all our traditions, ever reminding us to place principles before personalities."

With gratitude to our contributors, who generously shared their experiences of living with addiction or as the loved ones of addicts:

Aaron Eaves
Rev. Arvid Straube
Rev. Erin Splaine
Jane Davis
Rev. Jade "JD" Benson
Rev. Kathleen Rolenz
Rev. Leslie Takahashi
Rev. Lora Brandis
Rev. Lucas Hergert
Natalie Malter
Rev. Rebecca Bryan
Rev. Tandi Rogers

Thank you for taking this journey with us. Your gifts extend beyond what you will ever know. Thank you so much for your service.

January

Admitted that we were powerless

over our addiction—that our lives

had become unmanageable.

1

Be present, without judgement or regret,
without plans or expectations,
or even dreams,
And every moment
becomes a prayer.

—ELENA WESTBROOK

With pressure mounting on us as we face the year ahead, we recommit today to taking our recovery one day at a time. For this one day, I will not take part in behaviors or substances that trigger addiction. For this one day, I commit to caring for myself and to offering care to others. For this one day, I will get to a meeting, I will reach out to a sponsor, I will answer the phone if someone else reaches out to me. If you are struggling with addiction, let this be the day when you reach out to someone for help.

We know that, one day at a time, we remain present. One day at a time, we are able to build mindfulness and gratitude. One day at a time, we live out our faith and values, treating each person with dignity and respect, including ourselves. One day at a time, we live and thrive as human beings, as spiritual beings.

———————

Where do I find opportunities to live
in the moment right now?

Acceptance doesn't mean resignation; it means understanding that something is what it is and that there's got to be a way through it.

—MICHAEL J. FOX

Many years ago, when my mother was diagnosed with brain cancer, I didn't handle it well. Granted, I was aware of the many stages of grief, including shock, bargaining, and denial, but I hadn't yet addressed an overlying denial of addiction. Acknowledging it not only helped me come to terms with my mother's illness, but also gave me tools to accept life on its own terms.

Conceding to my innermost self that I had a problem, that my life as it was was chaotic and unruly, was the beginning of a life not of perfection, but of growth and beauty. Acceptance in all areas of daily living means that I don't need some sort of distraction from it to be at peace. If I know where I am, I can see where I need to go.

Am I ready to trust that I can find a way through whatever I face?

3

*We admitted we were powerless over our addiction—
that our lives had become unmanageable.*

—First Step

Step One, or more generally the act of acceptance, is often the hardest. Though we may readily admit that our lives have become unmanageable, we struggle with admitting we are powerless. Many of us take "powerless" to mean "helpless." And as competent, loving, moral, and devoted people, we understandably don't like to think of ourselves as helpless. We've been able to successfully manage the other aspects of our lives, why not this one?

However, the Twelve-Step program (or any other valid spiritual path) is not a path to helplessness. It is a path to empowerment. It is not disempowering to admit that our lives have become unmanageable, but it is disempowering to continue doing the same things and expecting different results. By admitting that we are powerless over this aspect of our lives, we are liberated from shame and from self-defeating repetition and empowered to take responsibility for what we actually have control over. And, maybe more importantly, we take the first step toward being able to ask for help.

What am I unwilling to accept in my life?
What would it be like to accept, without necessarily
approving of, this aspect of my life—just for today?

So let us give thanks for the broken places in our hearts, and in our lives.

—Rev. Thomas Rhodes

I sat on my couch that evening, after calling my sponsor to let her know I had relapsed. The feeling in my stomach was awful. I felt hollow, empty inside. For weeks, I had been telling myself I could handle this—it was just a little, light using, and not really a big deal. But here I was now, really facing it. I had relapsed. I was completely powerless.

For the last couple of weeks, I had been trying to hold it together, to not accept what was happening, to keep a good face on the outside when I was struggling on the inside. Keeping up appearances like this is exhausting. And I was feeling the exhaustion. I was tired. I felt hopeless. And I felt like a failure, like I had let myself and others down.

My sponsor recommended that I take some time to get honest with my Higher Power. So I sat still for a moment, really feeling that powerlessness. And in this meditation time, all I could feel was reassurance of God's love for me. It was an incredible feeling. It didn't make the pain go away, but it was a time for my Higher Power to let me know not to worry about our connection. It was as if God was saying, "My love is still here for you. I got this."

When is a time in my life that I have had to face my own human limitations?

5

It is confidence in our bodies, minds, and spirits that allows us to keep looking for new adventures.

—OPRAH WINFREY

I've watched some episodes of the television show *Queer Eye*, in which the goal of the stars is to make over folx regardless of their gender or sexual orientation. It has sometimes brought tears to my eyes, watching other people gather strength to be who they are meant to be rather than remain caught in societal or family expectations.

When I have looked in the mirror, or stepped on the scale, or given my opinion, I have been caught in a particular notion of what I am to be. Acceptance of who I truly am opens the world in front of me, rather than forcing me into self-imposed limitations.

Am I able to look in the mirror today
and like what I see?

Try something different. Surrender.
—RUMI

All religions, philosophies, and therapies include within them the principle of acceptance. Depending on the tradition, acceptance might be called surrender, detachment, letting go, actionless action, or any number of other things. Every tradition speaks of it because it is the single most transformative and empowering decision we can make—despite (or maybe because of) our culture's and ego's obsession with control.

Ultimately, the act of surrender is simply an affirmation of what is so. It acknowledges what the ego is (a helpful tool) and what the ego isn't (the source of our joy). It acknowledges what life is (something to enjoy and collaborate with) and what life isn't (something to control).

So, just for today, try something different. Try surrendering to your joy and to your pain. Surrender to your love, and surrender to that feeling when you know it's time to move on. Surrender to both your power and your need for help. Surrender to yourself, to the wisdom of those who truly love and support you, and to something greater than yourself.

———————

What one thing can I surrender to,
let go of, or accept today?

7

Here's a time, and here's another, when I laid down my fear and walked right on into it, right up to my neck into that roiling water.

—Rev. Victoria Safford

To let go of the control and accept that my father was an alcoholic was a huge ask. I had spent my life believing that the right words or the right actions might be able to keep him sober. I had been watching my mother and other family members doing everything in their power to get my dad to stop drinking. None of it had worked.

For a time, I had believed that by being the best child I could be, I could make things change. If I was quiet enough, if my grades were better, if I did things to make my father proud, maybe—just maybe—the drinking would stop. What I had to accept was that I didn't cause his addiction, I couldn't control his addiction, and nothing I could do would cure him of his addiction.

Accepting this was hard. And, once I got to a place of accepting that I couldn't do anything about his alcoholism, it was oddly freeing. I had been carrying a heavy burden all those years—a burden that was so good to just lay down. Trying to control things I can't control took a lot of energy. When I accepted there was nothing left for me to do, I could turn that energy elsewhere. I could begin the healing process I needed to go through.

Is there something I need to let go of in order to heal?

Maybe, sometimes, in the midst of things going terribly wrong, something is going just right.

—GERALD G. MAY

I love a new wall calendar. A new start to the school year. A new journal. A new computer. All are a blank slate, a way of saying, "You are worthy of another chance to begin again."

In recovery work, starting at the beginning may feel overwhelming or daunting, but it can also feel liberating. Like a brand new book, everything's possible, everything's new, and although there might be a bit of fear of the unknown, it's another way of saying all is well.

If it becomes clear that it's all too much, there's nothing wrong with starting at the beginning again. Take that fresh start.

———————

What is going right in my life today?

I naively thought that to solve this problem I'd have to let go, detach, and surrender once. Little did I know I'd be practicing these behaviors the rest of my life.

—MELODY BEATTIE

Accepting, detaching, and letting go are the work of a lifetime. Every time we truly surrender to life, we get relief, new insights, and a new freedom. However, we can often find ourselves riding a "pink cloud" after this new growth. Having reached a new mountaintop in our lives, it's easy to think we have reached *the* mountaintop. It's understandable to think that we must be done now!

However, as Melody Beattie points out, surrender is a lifelong process. It is not a single event, but instead is a way of life. There will be times in our lives when we will have to surrender every day, where we may have to make a First Step again. If this day is today for you, do not fret. Do not judge yourself as less than. Instead, take a breath and know that you are in good company, you are still on the path, and the next mountaintop will show itself to you. And you already know how to get there.

I know that in the past, I have detached and let go through times of trial and tribulation and grown from them. How can I let that knowing inform my actions today?

As I get older, the more I stay focused on the acceptance of myself and others, and choose compassion over judgment and curiosity over fear.

—Tracee Ellis Ross

I've been reminded over the years that I am not the one to determine whether someone around me has an addiction. Sometimes, observing a loved one's repeated unhealthy behavior, it is difficult not to make that judgment. But since I have control over my own behavior, I can choose to work with an attitude of compassion and look at others with curiosity rather than fear.

I find that I am the beneficiary of this healthier approach. If I don't dive into another's stress, I just may find true serenity.

Where have I been using judgment over compassion?

11

I didn't look.
Like you, I didn't look.
I turned my head,
Averted my eyes,
Plugged my ears,
Stilled my tongue.

—MARTHA KIRBY CAPO

Growing up Unitarian Universalist, the last place I wanted to talk about the complications of my parent's addiction was at church. Church was the place we went to look good. Church was a place where our home life remained secret.

So you could say church was one of the places where I learned denial. It was where I hid who I was. Sometimes it provided a helpful place to escape and just be myself. Other times it felt like a place where I couldn't bring the fullness of my experience. I looked around and, from my young perspective, no one else's families were having the same struggles we were.

Having a bit of perspective and time now, I have come to realize that other families were struggling with addiction too. It was just that no one was talking about it. I remember one of the people I grew up with telling me, when we were adults, about her mother's alcoholism. I had had no idea she was going through things similar to what I was. It left me wondering what might have happened if we had taken the risk to tell our stories rather than denying our truths.

———

Where are safe places for me to tell my story of addiction?

It is okay to be at a place of struggle. Struggle is just another word for growth.

—NEALE DONALD WALSCH

In the Jewish tradition, there is the story of Jacob who struggled and wrestled with the stranger in the night. Some say the stranger was an angel. Others say the stranger was God. And yet others say the stranger is a metaphor for Jacob's wrestling with himself. But whoever the stranger is, Jacob sticks with the struggle and demands a blessing. His hip is dislocated in the fight, but he receives his blessing, is renamed Israel ("he who struggles with God"), is reunited with his brother, and is better prepared to lead his community.

There's no denying that struggle is hard, uncomfortable, and something we would usually rather avoid. However, there's also no denying that struggle foreshadows almost every instance of growth in our individual and collective lives. So, just for today, have some compassion for yourself and know that within your struggle lies the key to your blessing and birthright.

———

How can I reframe my struggle today?
If my struggle were the bearer of my blessing,
how might I act differently?

13

Familiar things happen, and mankind does not bother about them. It requires a very unusual mind to undertake the analysis of the obvious.

—ALFRED NORTH WHITEHEAD

One of the best tools of my recovery has been to read and study Twelve-Step literature and then read it again with a sponsor, someone who has been dedicated to healing from destructive or unhealthy behavior for a longer period of time.

Over the years, I've made notes in the margins of my reading. I found one scrawled instruction, written years ago, that says, "Highlight things that sound familiar or that have happened." I'm reading a story that recalls a time about one hundred years ago, very unlike the time and place I live in. But if I look past the old-fashioned clothing and language, and look for similarities, I just might be able to connect.

In the "big book" of Alcoholics Anonymous, Bill describes how he assured his wife that "men of genius conceived their best projects when drunk." Bill's story reminds me of when my seminary professor suggested the best way to do theology was with a glass of scotch in hand. These days I'm not so sure that's true. Whitehead says it takes an unusual mind to analyze the obvious. It might take acceptance, too.

———

Is there something familiar right in front of me that I can now see?

May we trust that nothing will get worse for us
  putting that burden down for a moment.
May we let go of what weighs us down.
May we find that we can set down worry for longer
  and longer periods of time.

—REV. CAROL ALLMAN-MORTON

Power is the illusion that we can maintain control. Control over what? Doesn't really matter. Control over other people, control over a situation, control over whether or not I pick up the drugs, the food, the alcohol, or whatever I use today—it is all an illusion. We have no power. We have no control over anything but our own actions.

To admit powerlessness, to admit that our lives have become unmanageable, is a forever thing. There will not be a time when I gain power back. There will not be a time when my life is suddenly manageable.

It may sound hopeless at first. But to accept this reality is freeing. It allows us the space to really face reality as it is. Because when I keep chasing that power, that control, that manageability, I am chasing after something that cannot be caught. I am chasing after an illusion.

Embrace the freedom. Embrace the powerlessness. Accept your situation wherever you are. And may the truth of it all set you free.

Where am I attempting to exert control today? How
can I let some of this illusion go?

The question is not how to get cured, but how to live.
—JOSEPH CONRAD

Working a program of recovery is not about finding a magic wand or silver bullet that will forever free us from our struggles. Recovery is about finding a new way of life, a way of life that actually works for us, our relationships, and our world.

Of course, some find this disheartening. The idea of forever identifying as an addict, alcoholic, codependent, etc. can feel like defeat. But this couldn't be further from the truth.

Accepting that there is no one-time solution or cure to our unique struggles (i.e., our humanity) opens the door for self-compassion, the ability to ask for help, and keeps us honest. It encourages us not to look for easy answers but instead to pursue a way of life that can carry us through good times and bad times. It invites us into a way of life that honors all that we have been, all that we are, and all that we are meant to be.

In what ways am I trying to "fix" myself, other people, or a situation? Is there a way that I can show up, with compassion and integrity, without trying to fix anything?

Families are messy. Immortal families are eternally messy. Sometimes the best we can do is to remind each other that we're related for better or for worse . . . and try to keep the maiming and killing to a minimum.

—RICK RIORDAN

I decided to build my family tree on a popular genealogy site. Not all of it was easy. I noted foster care placements, divorces, and remarriages on both sides of my family. Much of my biological family's history was unknown. Some of what I discovered in census records made clear that there was addiction, abandonment, and loss.

Looking through all this in one place, one family tree, brought to mind memories and a feeling of wondering what happened in the areas I can't know. Afterward I was filled with both sadness and gratitude.

Acceptance is a process. I feel that I've accepted my disease, but I sometimes have to start over again when I need to accept my family as it is, accepting the losses that I cannot change. I would much rather have this understanding than not.

Have I truly accepted that I have a problem?
Can I look at the messiness of my family with peace?

17

Spirit of great mystery, hear the still, small voice in me.

—SHELLEY JACKSON DENHAM

If we get still enough, we can find acceptance. It is inside of us, a part of our deeper knowing. It is what our Higher Power (however we choose to define "Higher Power") wants for us. Acceptance. Acceptance of our thoughts, our actions, our ways of being in the world, and even our addictions.

But we begin with getting still enough to listen. It is the disease talking when we hear that we are not doing enough or that we need to do more to be productive or worthy. It is the disease talking when we hear that we have to push through and keep going. To disobey and become still helps us to listen to ourselves with acceptance. It helps us to know that what we are doing, how we are being, is enough for this moment.

To know acceptance is to know freedom. It is freedom from a tape playing in our heads over and over again, saying that we are not good enough or not worthy or not whatever. It is freedom to extend acceptance to others out of accepting ourselves. It is freedom to just listen and accept what comes. May you know such a freedom.

———

When can I find five or ten minutes today to embrace stillness?

I don't have to have faith, I have experience.
—JOSEPH CAMPBELL

The beauty of the Twelve-Step program, and other programs of recovery, is that you are not required to believe anything to work the program. There is no creed you must confess in order to have access to the life-saving grace of recovery. Instead of specific beliefs, you are invited into a community and a practice. You are invited to experience its effects for yourself and define things like "Higher Power" and "recovery" in a way that makes sense to you.

If faith means belief without evidence, that is not what is required. If faith means the willingness to try something new, to try working a program that has produced results for others, and to draw your own conclusions, then that is the faith that is asked for here. It is a faith built upon your own willingness and experience—a faith that is available for all.

———

Just for today, can I ground myself in my spiritual practice and networks of support? Can I let my beliefs and faith arise naturally from these experiences?

19

Love yourself first and everything else falls into line.
You really have to love yourself to get anything done
in this world.

—LUCILLE BALL

We're living in an age of overwhelm. Not just with minor things like our many yogurt choices, but with work expectations, late-stage capitalism, and white supremacy culture. Which thing do I do first? How do I set priorities? What do I do when things go wrong?

Acceptance is the key to all my problems. I can move into acceptance only when I begin to love myself, when I believe I am worthy of the effort, when I pay attention to my health and well-being before the next bullet point on the to-do list.

It might feel like loving yourself can only be put lower on the list, that it is the result of accomplishment. But if I put loving myself first, I can realize the essentials of living, knowing what really matters.

Plus, I can't get anything done, even the trivial, if I don't love myself first.

What words could I write on my bathroom mirror
to remind me every morning that I'm worth it?

The inherent worth and dignity of every person.
—FIRST PRINCIPLE OF
UNITARIAN UNIVERSALISM

The First Principle of Unitarian Universalism applies to all people. It goes back to the universal love that our Universalist heritage tells us is accessible to all and to the respect for every person that our Unitarian heritage emphasizes. Of the Seven Principles that Unitarian Universalism is grounded in, it is perhaps the one most often referred to. And yet, sometimes it is not always reflected in our actions or our words.

The inherent worth and dignity of every person should be honored and respected, even—and especially—those of addicts. We have struggled to see our own worth and dignity at times. At other times, when our egos are inflated and running amok, we see our worth and dignity so very clearly, while losing sight of that of others. In our recovery programs, it is often said that addicts are egomaniacs with a self-esteem issue. We fluctuate between thinking only of ourselves and thinking we are the worst.

Knowledge of our own inherent worth and dignity does not come from a place of power over people, nor from a place of self-deprecation. It means accepting our story, getting our ego right-sized, and recognizing exactly where we have personal power and where we have lost the power to choose.

How can I embrace my own inherent worth and dignity in the next twenty-four hours?

We cannot selectively numb emotions. When we numb the painful emotions, we also numb the positive emotions.

—BRENÉ BROWN

When we engage in our addictive behaviors, we are almost always trying to numb negative emotions. These negative emotions could be anything from trauma reactions to the everyday experiences of stress and anxiety. At first, the behavior seems like the perfect fix. Just a little of this or that to take the edge off of the depression, help keep the anxiety at bay, and allow us to at least appear normal.

Unfortunately, numbing isn't selective. When we numb any emotions, we numb all emotions. What starts off as an escape route becomes a trap that sucks us in deeper and deeper the more we try to escape through it. Moving into acceptance, taking the First Step of admitting that we are powerless over these emotions and that our lives have become unmanageable, frees us from this trap. It opens us back up to all of our emotions. It allows us to learn how to live life on life's terms, making possible a more integrated, more authentic, and richer life than we've ever known.

What if I held my own difficult feelings with the same compassion I offer to my loved ones? What if I knew that there is much more to me than these feelings and that these feelings still need to be heard?

Keep your First Step close.
　—RECOVERY SAYING

Long ago, when I was newer in my recovery from addiction, I had a friend in the program, someone I admired, who, although the same age as me, had thirteen years of sobriety. He was well known, seemingly popular at meetings, and seemed to say the right things. A year after I met him, he took his own life.

Addiction is very complicated stuff, and my friend likely had some other undiagnosed illness accompanying his alcoholism, but I'm so often reminded of how important it is to remember how I got here.

It is said in the "big book" of Alcoholics Anonymous that "acceptance is the answer to *all* my problems today. When I am disturbed, it is because I find some person, place, thing, or situation—some fact of my life—unacceptable to me, and I can find no serenity until I accept that person, place, thing, or situation as being exactly the way it is supposed to be at this moment."

Today, I will remember that the first step in recovery is to admit I am powerless over my addiction.

---

*What are some ways I can visit my
First Step today?*

23

We cast not our eyes below, we say to ourselves we are how we came, wounded from struggles, triumphant in our survival, entitled by birthright to belong to this the only humankind there is, saying I am included, I belong, I am here, and I will be and do.

—Rev. Ma Theresa Gustilo Gallardo

We have made it so far. We who have been touched by addiction: we have survived the many nights of worry, the days of wondering what we could do, and the times when we were just resigned to let things happen because we were tired of fighting. Our bodies have been through so much, our spirits have endured so many cycles of swearing off it, only to return again. We have survived so much.

And perhaps you are still surviving. Perhaps you are still in the midst of an addictive relationship or an addiction to alcohol, food, drugs, love, work, or whatever your substance might be. At some point, the survival mode becomes exhausting. This is the best time to reach out for help—when we are desperate for it.

Claim your chair. Claim your story. Accept what you have been through to get here. Accept the help because it is the only way for us to survive to see another day. Remember how many have not made it to really living—to thriving, even. We have made it so far.

---

*Where in my life am I surviving,
and where am I thriving?*

*At fifteen life had taught me undeniably that
surrender, in its place, was as honorable as resistance,
especially if one had no choice.*

—MAYA ANGELOU

There are times in life when we must resist. We must resist the oppression of ourselves and others. We must resist the temptation to act when we know we are not grounded in our best selves. Resistance and struggle can be holy acts, expressions of our deepest love for ourselves, our communities, and that which we call holy.

And there are times in life when we must surrender. There are some things in life and in ourselves that we simply do not have control over. In these cases, the most effective, honest, and faithful response we can offer is to surrender to what is so. Our powerlessness over our addiction, other people's feelings and actions, and the ultimate outcome of events are places for surrender. In these cases, surrender does not mean defeat. It simply means that we yield to a power greater than ourselves, accepting and honoring that this problem is too big for us to solve alone.

---

*How can I be mindful today of the dance between
resistance and surrender? When faced with a problem,
troublesome feeling, or situation, how will I remind
myself to ask which will be more faithful and effective:
to resist or to yield?*

25

Compassion requires us to be weak with the weak, vulnerable with the vulnerable, and powerless with the powerless. Compassion means full immersion in the condition of being human.

—Fr. Henri Nouwen

As part of working Step One in Adult Children of Alcoholics, I made a chart of all of my family members, tracking where addiction and dysfunction had been present. At first, it was overwhelming to look at. How could all of this have happened in my family? Here, laid bare on the paper, were many of the family secrets I had been encouraged to never tell.

When I shared this chart of my family with my sponsor, they showed me that this chart was a way to admit my own powerlessness. With the prevalent addiction and abuse in my family, I could not have turned out any different. And they shared that their family chart was quite similar— so many of us had similar behavior patterns passed down through the generations. In this tender act of vulnerability, what I had held as shameful suddenly became a source of self-compassion.

For years, I had tried to fix my family or cover up the parts I didn't want others to see. But in writing it all out, I realized I was powerless over the effects of growing up in a family with addiction. My life was not a mistake or a shameful secret; it just was what it was. What a profound sense of freedom!

Where can I find compassion for my past experiences so that I can live more freely in the present?

We will not regret the past nor wish to shut the door on it.

> —*ALCOHOLICS ANONYMOUS,*
> "THE BIG BOOK"

So many promises can come true for those in recovery if they will simply use the spiritual practice of "working the program."

Remembering what happened, unfortunate events to which I contributed in a negative way, does not keep me in shame but reminds me to live a life of integrity and thoughtfulness.

My past doesn't define me, but instead helps me see where I've come from. I have worked with a sponsor, and I shared with that person the things that made me feel less than. I have made amends. I have a level of acceptance that now lets me find joy in my life.

———————

Is there something in my past that keeps me from a joyful acceptance?

27

Come, come, whoever you are.
Wanderer, worshipper, lover of leaving.
Ours is no caravan of despair.
Come, yet again, come.

—RUMI

Unitarian Universalists sometimes sing a hymn with these lyrics from Rumi. They always remind me of the saying in the "big book" of Alcoholics Anonymous that "we are like the passengers of a great liner the moment after rescue from shipwreck when camaraderie, joyousness and democracy pervade the vessel from steerage to Captain's table." Other folks may find it odd, but there is a joy in the fellowship of our recovery programs, a feeling as if we have survived a shipwreck, and deep relief to be there.

Before getting into recovery, I thought that it would be difficult and joyless. But the work of recovery is for everyone who wants to work it—no exceptions. And there is deep joy there alongside the pain and all of the difficult feelings. To recover only takes willingness to do the work to put our substances down and pick up a recovery program. There are people who want to help, who will welcome us in after the shipwreck to a caravan filled with joy, ready to take us to a new future.

Where have I experienced a shipwreck along my
life's journey? Where have I been able to find my
way to a caravan of hope?

There are all kinds of addicts, I guess. We all have pain.
And we all look for ways to make the pain go away.

—SHERMAN ALEXIE

Terminal uniqueness is a common presumption among people who suffer from addiction. We think we are unique because we believe that there is no way that anyone else could be experiencing what we are experiencing. It's terminal because this kind of thinking can be deadly.

Having worked in addiction for several years, having been surrounded by it my whole life, and in working through my own struggles, I have come to believe that addiction is best understood as the human condition . . . amplified. As Sherman Alexie points out, we all (in one way or another) look for ways to take the edge off.

So you are not alone in this. And that is why recovery programs and spiritualities that focus on relationships (to a community, a mentor, and something larger than yourself) are so effective. They are effective because they thrust us out of our false beliefs of separation and into an experience of the truth of who we are: inextricably connected to the rest of this human family and the very spirit of life.

Just for today, can I trust that there are people out
there who could empathize and support me in my
life? If I already know who they are, can I give them
a call or visit today? And if I don't, can I pick a
local support group and give them a try?

29

Acceptance of what has happened is the first step to overcoming the consequences of any misfortune.

—WILLIAM JAMES

Recovery from addiction has the added benefit of helping me look with clear eyes at the original sin of our nation, slavery. Rather than seeing what happened in 1619 as separate from me, I am able to see my part, and better realize the consequences of that long-ago action.

Rather than finding the problem of racism completely overwhelming, I am willing to take one step at a time to acknowledge it and become part of the solution.

Tink Tinker, a member of the Osage Nation and a renowned expert in American Indian cultures, history, and religious traditions, referred to America as a "dry drunk" because it wasn't willing to take part in a program of recovery. I want to be a healthy member of community and find serenity.

How might I apply my recovery to an antiracist future?

We learned we had to fully concede to our innermost selves that we were alcoholics. This is the first step in recovery. The delusion that we are like other people, or presently may be, has to be smashed.

—*ALCOHOLICS ANONYMOUS*,
"THE BIG BOOK"

One of the major parts of the First Step is to accept that we can never safely use that food, alcohol, or substance. For me, this was hard. I had been living in a state of compulsive overeating for most of my life. The thinking that somehow, someday, I would be able to control it was always my downfall. It was what led to relapse each of the times I went there.

To accept that we are powerless over something means we no longer have a choice. When we are powerless over alcohol, that first drink leads to many more drinks. When we are powerless over food, that first compulsive bite leads to many more bites.

It may sound grim, but it is the starting point. It is the place we need to begin. And it is freeing to no longer live in the illusion of control that never works. By accepting that we are powerless over our substances, we can take all the energy we were using to try to control our use of those substances and direct it toward healing from our addictions.

What am I powerless over, and where have I been seeking control?

31

If you desire healing, let yourself fall ill.
Let yourself fall ill.

—RUMI

Many of us have internalized self-defeating narratives around illness. Some of these are religious messages that tell us that sickness is a sign that we are out of alignment with the spirit. Others come from our culture that tells us that sickness is a sign of laziness. If we only tried harder, had tougher skin, or made different decisions, we wouldn't be in the mess that we're in. Either way, the message is clear: If you're sick, it's your fault.

Admittedly, we are not completely powerless over our health. Our decisions do make an impact on our quality of life. However, until we are ready to acknowledge that something is wrong, we prevent ourselves from receiving the healing that we seek. So admitting that something is wrong and "letting ourselves fall ill" is one of the most powerful decisions we will ever make. It is quite literally the First Step to recovery.

———————

Is there an area of my life that I am trying to "tough
through," but the struggle doesn't seem to be going
away? Is it time to surrender, let myself fall ill,
and open myself up to a new way of life?

February

STEP TWO: HOPE,

OPEN-MINDEDNESS

Came to believe that a power

greater than ourselves could

restore us to sanity.

For some of us, it's safer to believe there's something wrong with us than to be aware of the reality of our lives.

—STEPHANIE S. COVINGTON

I have been in many situations where I've asked myself, "Am I insane?" Whether the question is prompted by the behavior of my family of origin, behaviors in a congregation, or living in a culture built on genocide, abuse, and oppression, real insanity, is, as Stephanie Covington says, "being disconnected from your own reality."

Denial is only safe for so long.

My Unitarian Universalist faith provides tools to connect me to a larger reality, but I am wise to remember that a spiritual practice, such as meditation or a regular spiritual meeting, keeps me grounded. It provides the strength to do what I need to do, to make a change in my situation, to make a change in myself.

Is there some reality in my life that makes it unmanageable? Where am I finding strength to acknowledge the truth?

Once upon a time we were
Now we are
And some day (Hallelujah!) we shall surely become
Amen

—MARGARET BRAXTON WILLIAMS

One of the greatest gifts of being alive is change. While change can at times feel overwhelming and scary, it is the very force that enables us to grow into who we are meant to be. It is the possibility of change in each new day that gives us hope for the future. Although there will always be the truth of who we have been in the past, the opportunity to learn and to be transformed opens us up to a new way forward. No longer must we feel stuck in the cycles that cause us pain. We can give ourselves over to another way of being. We can discover hope.

This process of becoming who we are meant to be is not easy. We must be gentle with ourselves as we stumble into the unknown on our journey toward recovery. There are no easy answers in this place of mystery and healing. There are only time, mistakes, learning, and more time. On this day, may we summon the courage to turn toward change and celebrate the hope alive in the possibilities awaiting us just around the corner.

How might my choices today empower me to grow
even more deeply into who I am meant to be?

3

Direct experience of that transcending mystery and wonder, affirmed in all cultures, which moves us to a renewal of the spirit and an openness to the forces that create and uphold life.

—First Source of Unitarian Universalism

A sponsee and I were beginning work on Step Two. As we talked through what a Higher Power could be, she said something like "I'm replacing the false hope of the food [*our addictive substance*] with the real hope of God." It was a profound learning for me. The work we are doing in recovery is finding a hope of substance, a relationship of deep and growing trust with something more important than we are.

This ties in so well with the First Source of Unitarian Universalism! In Step Two, we become willing to have direct experience of transcending mystery and wonder. We are not asked to decide what the mystery and wonder is. We are simply asked to be open and to take hope that there is more out there than the addictions that we face and methods we have developed of controlling and moderating and treating the deep wound of spiritual emptiness with whatever substance we are addicted to. We are replacing the false hope of managing and someday controlling our addictions with the real hope that there is something larger out there that wants to help us, that loves us at our very core without our having to do a thing to earn that love.

Has there been a moment when I believed I was beyond being loved? Where do I find love today?

Beauty is a mystery, but no one knows it anymore.
The recipes, the secrets are forgotten.

—EDGAR DEGAS

I recently heard a suggestion that, in the turbulent times in which we live, we should be working at about 60 percent in order to be ready to handle the trauma when it comes. I'm not sure it's even possible to work 60 percent in a time where our usual practice is 110 percent, but I get the point. There must be time when we can look for beauty, when we can explore personal and community spirituality, when we may practice peace.

I need to remind myself, especially when I'm not traveling, to visit the special exhibits at the art museum. I don't have to be on vacation to take in creativity and inspiration. Let us remember to offer ourselves space to learn, to be, and to find opportunities to open our heart.

Where might I discover and appreciate beauty?
How might I find places to rest my spirit so that
I'm ready when needed?

5

Pour yourself out like a fountain.
Flow into the knowledge that what you are seeking
finishes often at the start, and, with ending, begins.
—RAINER MARIA RILKE

A choice to change our lives, to seek a path of healing, is a choice tangled around beginnings and endings. When we summon the courage to turn our lives over to the journey of recovery, we begin to discover many new gifts surrounding us—serenity, courage, and wisdom. And we also come to realize that there are things and people we must leave behind as we begin the process of rediscovering and nurturing our truest selves. Yet amid the pain of these partings lie the seeds of new possibilities, of a safe and healthy self-love that we have not known before.

The story of choosing recovery is a story of encountering grief, for all that we have lost along the way and for all that we must still leave behind. Opening ourselves up to our sadness, accepting its place in our healing process, gives us the space we need to mourn with honesty and to learn to love ourselves in a new way. There is hope alive amid the loss, healing on the other side of the pain. And while we must leave some people behind, we find a whole new community, our recovery community, supporting and loving us as we are, through it all.

What or who am I still carrying with me that
I need to let go of? Can I find time today to give
myself a few minutes to honor my grief?

I cannot believe in a God who wants to be praised all the time.

—FRIEDRICH NIETZSCHE

I find it so wonderful to be a Unitarian Universalist, invited to consider the concept of God in so many ways, all of which are acceptable. Twelve-Step programs have a reputation for requiring theistic views of a "higher power" and are filled with old-fashioned theistic language. But they have also brought me to an open-mindedness through which I can both sit in rooms with people who believe differently than I do and envision a Higher Power that is not synonymous with traditional concepts of God.

I remember years ago, at a ministers' gathering, one colleague used to wear a T-shirt that said, "'God is dead.'— Nietzsche." Below that it said, "'Nietzsche is dead.'—God." Though it was obviously meant as a humorous statement, I got stuck, not accepting the humor. Years have passed and my maturity has increased. I still agree with Nietzsche, not believing in a God who wants to be praised, but I have come to believe that God doesn't really need praising. We need to praise, to acknowledge something that reminds us that we are not the center of the world.

What bit of open-mindedness
might I discover today?

A free and responsible search for truth and meaning.
—FOURTH PRINCIPLE OF
UNITARIAN UNIVERSALISM

Step Two reads, "Came to believe that a power greater than ourselves could restore us to sanity." As Unitarian Universalists, some of us came to this Step naturally, with a previously established relationship with a Higher Power. For others of us, this concept was a struggle. Why should I need a Higher Power to restore me to sanity? Who is this Higher Power? How do I reconcile being an atheist with being in recovery?

Happily, a program of recovery encourages us to seek a Higher Power of our own understanding, whether it is one outside of ourselves or one found in human beings, a recovery group, or a certain state of human consciousness. No one is going to tell us what to believe and how to be in relationship with a Higher Power. It is up to us.

What we acknowledge in Step Two is that we are in need of help from something greater than our individual selves. Left to our own devices, we have been struggling. We have acted in ways that were not sane, resorting to desperate measures to try to quit or even to try to make someone else quit. We are in need of help from a Higher Power so we will never have to be alone in our addiction again.

---

*How do I connect with something
greater than myself?*

When we become aware that we've forgotten the wounded child in ourselves, we feel great compassion for that child.

—THICH NHAT HANH

Opening ourselves up to recovery requires remembering the wounded child who lives within us, the child who is still scared and hurting from years of neglect. Although we may have tried to ignore or silence our inner child through our addiction and dysfunctional behaviors, that child has always been with us, longing for our care and love. Our recovery can only truly begin when we are willing to stop running from ourselves and acknowledge the pain that our inner child carries.

While we may not have received the love we needed and deserved as children, we know that we can learn to give ourselves that love as adults. No longer must we live in the damaging cycle of self-abandonment. No longer do we need to distract ourselves from the work of healing. We have the tools we need to begin our recovery right here. This recovery is—at its core—a process of re-parenting ourselves with kindness, healthy boundaries, and abundant love. What our inner wounded children most need is for us to embrace them and say, "I love you. You are not alone. You are safe now. I am here."

————————

Suppose I take a deep, calming breath and imagine myself as a young child. How can I be kind to that child today? How can I honor their preciousness with inner love?

*The natural flights of the human mind are not
from pleasure to pleasure, but from hope to hope.*
—SAMUEL JOHNSON

I love these words of Samuel Johnson, especially because he suggests "natural flights." Might I deduce that it's not natural to go from pleasure to pleasure? Part of the destructiveness of addiction is that it expects pleasure to be the natural state of things. There was a time when I thought life was wrong when it wasn't providing me with a pleasurable experience. I became anxious and overwhelmed when things were difficult, and I couldn't sit with monotony or even quiet.

That craving for pleasure, or endorphins, may be normal in the same way that disease is normal, but it is not the place I want to be anymore. I am more content to live with hope, and not to visit it in a fleeting leap but to settle into it with serenity and peace.

―――――――

What does hope mean for me today?

There is a principle which is a bar against all information, which is proof against all arguments, and which cannot fail to keep a man in everlasting ignorance—that principle is contempt prior to investigation.

—HERBERT SPENCER

As a Unitarian Universalist, I always thought I was open-minded. Being raised in this faith, I was taught to honor each person's inherent worth and dignity alongside their own search for truth and meaning. Getting into recovery revealed to me just how closed-minded I had been.

When actions were suggested to me, I often found myself wondering if what I was doing could really work. I saw all these folks around the table with me in whom it had worked, and still I was skeptical. But the further I grew, and the more I stayed with the work of recovery, the more I saw that these thoughts were not helpful.

I was engaging in "contempt prior to investigation," meaning I was not open to the learning and the growth that could happen along the way. When I truly became desperate for help, it was a gift. The gift was a willingness and an open-mindedness, a readiness to try anything to see if it would work. And this mindset is what has ultimately led me to the deepest healing of my life: the gift of recovery.

Where has my skepticism got in the way of learning something new?

11

No, I'd never been to this country before. No, I didn't know where the roads would lead me. No, I didn't intend to turn back.

—MARY OLIVER

Beginning the work of recovery leads us into many unknown places. While we had grown accustomed to living in the cycle of destruction, isolation, and despair, in our recovery we come to see that peace, community, and hope are possible. We can choose another road. This choice, to leave behind our familiar patterns of behavior, is not an easy one. It demands great courage to let go of what we know. And it is a choice that requires loving patience with ourselves as we stumble and take wrong turns along this new way we have chosen.

Although it is difficult work, we wake up every day and rededicate ourselves to the new road ahead of us. We ask for help—from our recovery communities, from our Higher Power—because we know that we cannot and do not need to journey alone. We know, from listening to the stories of the courageous fellow travelers who have gone this way before us, that healing is possible. And even as so much in our lives remains uncertain, we make the brave decision to choose self-love, trying to trust that there is a vibrant, beautiful life awaiting us, as we continue forward in this journey.

Who in my recovery community can I reach out to today, if I am feeling lonely? How might asking for support when I need it help to nourish my spirit?

Anxious systems also fail to get a clear view of things. Embedded in their dread, they lose a sense of proportion. They have little awareness of what is happening and how it is being mutually maintained.

—PETER L. STEINKE

Years ago, I heard church systems consultant Peter Steinke talk about how important it is for leaders to "get on the balcony," meaning to get an overview of a whole situation. These days we call that ability to see a whole picture *systems sensibility*. It is a competency that enables us to realize that we are all interconnected and interrelated, that a change to one part can affect all other parts. It lets us understand mental models and look at our own.

As I was talking to a friend about balcony views, she mentioned to me the concept of "balcony people," people who cheer on others. If you are a balcony person you help lift others up rather than bring them down. We each need balcony people in our life, to offer realistic hope and possibility.

When I think of taking a balcony view of the system of which I am a part, I have a better opportunity to see the positive, to find the health, to not become mired in the negative. I have a greater chance of becoming a balcony person to others.

Am I able to take the larger view from the balcony? Who are the balcony people who support me?

13

and here you are living
despite it all
     —RUPI KAUR

We are still here. We are still here. We are still here. Even after all that we have been through, we have survived to this present moment. And because of this inner strength, we know that we are resilient. Today we honor this resilience inside of us, remembering that it will help us in our journey to recovery. We take a moment to breathe deeply and offer gratitude for our bodies and our spirits, which have brought us to this place.

Although we often come into recovery wanting fast solutions to our problems, we soon realize that there are no quick fixes to the predicament of being human in this messy, complex world. While some days we still feel shattered and disappointed, falling short and letting down others and ourselves, we continue to show up and try again. We do our best to make healthy choices, knowing that we will continue to make mistakes and that it will be okay. Instead of aspiring to perfection, we dedicate our lives to the never-ending process of learning, doing so with patience and an open heart. We remember that having more work to do is not a sign of failure. We remember that having more work to do is what it means to be alive.

———————

What about myself am I grateful for today? Can I take
a moment to offer a prayer of gratitude for the resilient
body and spirit that have brought me all this way?

We believe that each person must be free to search for what is true and right in life.

> —UNITARIAN UNIVERSALISM'S
> PRINCIPLES IN SIMPLER LANGUAGE

The first sponsor I worked with was a pagan woman who believed in multiple gods and goddesses. I was so grateful we were working together, as I had explored earth-based traditions in my Unitarian Universalist community. When we spoke of a Higher Power together, her definitions were so expansive. She turned to different deities in different times of her life for spiritual support and guidance.

One of the initial barriers I faced in Twelve-Step recovery was my belief that the people I was with in "the rooms" didn't believe in the same thing I believed in. Their reliance on a God that could restore them to sanity seemed counter to my Unitarian Universalist theology. What about human free will? What about our power to choose?

My sponsor emphasized that we are invited to find a Higher Power of our own understanding. What was important was that there was a Higher Power at work in the world and it was not me. My relationship with this power was entirely personal, one that I could trust and rely on for the hard road ahead. Through this perspective, my mind opened up, and I could finally identify with this program in a way that was informed by my Unitarian Universalist values.

What is more important than I am?

15

I like the night. Without the dark, we'd never see the stars.

—STEPHENIE MEYER

I am continually informed by Sharon Welch's "feminist ethic of risk," that notion that those who engage in justice struggles always do so from a position of incomplete understanding and limited perspective.

I am reminded that despair comes from a place of privilege. I want to be grounded in communities of hope and resistance.

By staying connected to a spiritual practice of recovery, I stay connected to hope, to open-mindedness, and I realize that despair is a privilege I cannot afford.

———————

How can I see hope in the dark?

Hope rises. It rises from the heart of life, here and now,
beating with joy and sorrow. Hope longs. It longs for
good to be affirmed, for justice and love to prevail, for
suffering to be alleviated, and for life to flourish in
peace. . . . Hope acts—to bless, to protect, and to repair.

—REV. REBECCA PARKER AND
REV. JOHN BUEHRENS

Hope. It's a word that we hear so often, and yet so few of us understand its true meaning. Does it mean that we're always supposed to feel happy? Does it mean that we have all the answers already figured out? No. Although hope is often mistaken for optimism, hope is far more complex. While optimism suggests a kind of irrepressible certainty that everything will be okay in the end, hope invites us instead to inhabit the place beyond certainty. Hope holds room for our despair and our loss, even as it challenges us to envision a different kind of future.

Recovery, like hope, is not simple. It is not a place that we wander into passively but rather one we choose to enter into willfully, as we begin to reach out and ask for help from our Higher Power and our community. It is not something we can do alone: we need one another to do this work. On this day, we remind ourselves that we can always turn to our recovery community for support, as we try to make sense of the joys and sorrows on this path of healing.

How does hope help me to approach the work
of recovery?

17

Hold fast to dreams
For if dreams die
Life is a broken-winged bird
That cannot fly.

—LANGSTON HUGHES

I remember, at some point in my childhood, being required to memorize poetry. One I still recall is the brief poem "Dreams," by Langston Hughes. It's hard to imagine how this poem affected me as a child, except that it stayed with me, and it seems like, whenever times are hard, I find it easy to pull these words, as well as Emily Dickinson's poem "Hope is the thing with feathers," to the front of my mind.

When we're in the throes of addiction, hope can feel like a ridiculous concept. Despair seems so much more plausible. But I have found that to be self-centered thinking. The poets remind me to "hold fast to dreams, for when dreams go, life is a barren field, frozen with snow."

In recovery, hope is not a wistful notion but an actionable one. When I keep doing the next right thing, I am hopeful.

How might the poets guide me?
What hopeful act is right in front of me?

History, despite its wrenching pain
Cannot be unlived, but if faced with courage,
Need not be lived again.

—MAYA ANGELOU

We have often heard the saying that "history repeats itself." The repetition of history is something we have witnessed personally in the grief and pain that have been inherited over the course of generations in our families of origin. We know that addiction impacts not only individuals but also whole families, as dysfunctional behaviors are passed down from one generation to the next. Some days the "wrenching pain" of our own familial stories can feel overwhelming. How do we stay hopeful in the midst of this history? How do we change the system by changing our own lives?

We must begin by acknowledging our past. When we recognize our own histories, we can begin to move forward in a new way. Our present and our future need not be determined wholly by who we have been or where we have come from. In recovery we find the tools we need to begin to release ourselves from the generational pain we carry, cultivating healthier behaviors from a place of courage, humility, and love. We root our hope in this place—in the power of the present moment and in the possibilities for the future that lie ahead.

What small but important choice can I make for myself today to help me in my recovery journey?

19

It is possible to become discouraged about the injustice we see everywhere. But God did not promise us that the world would be humane and just. He gives us the gift of life and allows us to choose the way we will use our limited time on earth. It is an awesome opportunity.

—CÉSAR CHÁVEZ

Hope is not foolish wishful thinking. It is a desire for things to be better. And our own free will, what we choose, is action that makes hope real. But something has to change on our part in order to make hope active, not simply longing.

Seeing and hearing others' experience is one of the great tenets of recovery. The fellowship and wisdom offered through recovery groups makes hope available, creates new thoughts and ways of seeing things that can make hope real.

When I first decided to enter recovery from addiction, I didn't really realize that's what I was doing. Each move I made brought more clarity and a better day. My action in recovery is what has led to a changed life. It has offered me an "awesome opportunity."

What choice can I make today to make hope come alive?

If we did not learn self-love in our youth, there is still hope. The light of love is always in us, no matter how cold the flame. It is always present, waiting for the spark to ignite, waiting for the heart to awaken.

—BELL HOOKS

In the midst of the challenges that we faced with addiction and dysfunction, we often came to feel isolated, from others and from ourselves. Our truest self was forsaken by our self-sabotaging choices, which only led us toward greater despair and loneliness. Sometimes we found ourselves wondering who we really were amid the chaos and confusion that had come to rule our lives. We wondered if we might have lost our authentic self along the way.

Although we may have forgotten our truest selves, we learn in recovery that we can still remember our way back to them. This is, in fact, the true meaning of "to recover." As we begin to rescue what was lost or taken from us, we find ourselves anew. We reclaim our lives and regain a sense of wholeness, by slowly learning to release the years of fear and shame that have held us back. As we begin to heal our wounds, we stop hiding from the world, and we start to live our lives from a place of greater honesty and compassion. We come to understand that we are worthy of love just as we are. We are enough. We are so much more than enough.

When do I feel most in touch with my truest self? What kinds of places, experiences, and people help me feel connected and seen for who I am?

21

Occasionally we rouse from our trance to remember our wholeness. For a time we embody unsentimental love.

—REV. CHIP ROUSH

The phrase "restore us to sanity" in the Second Step implies that there is something wrong with us to begin with. However, there are many people with mental illness who live full, beautiful lives. It is helpful to know that in feeling an obsessive drive toward an addictive substance that harms us, we are not alone. So many live with impulses to harm themselves.

As a child growing up in an alcoholic home, I spent years believing there was something I could do, some behavior I could embrace, some magic words that would change how my alcoholic parent drank. This belief led me into some pretty irrational behavior and patterns of thought.

I am grateful today to be able to talk about these patterns of thought and behavior with others who have been there too. That is one of the saving messages of Unitarian Universalism: we are not alone.

Today, being "restored to sanity" means talking with others who understand me. It's the beginning of being able to heal from these behaviors and thoughts, so that I'm not trying to act a certain way to get the things that I want. It's putting the things I learned into perspective. I was a child then. I am an adult now.

Where is there an opportunity on this day for me to share with someone and receive an understanding presence?

Where there is great love there are always miracles.
—WILLA CATHER

My spouse was watching a charity golf tournament on TV. The organization being benefited by the contest was a cancer hospital with "Hope" in its name. A young teen who was a participant in the tournament was being interviewed for the TV viewers. Instead of offering a trite definition of hope, they described it as being about relationships.

How wise, I thought, to be assured that we could find hope through making connections, through caring, through honesty and commitment. And although that young teen might have been thinking about hopeful relationships when a loved one has cancer, building relationships is essential when recovering from addiction or dealing with a family member who is recovering.

Helpful slogans like "let go and let God" might sound trite, but they are a reminder that I can still be connected in relationship without solving all of someone else's problems. Great love does not mean managing someone's life for them. I'm learning not to suffer because of the actions of someone else. I believe hope is about relationships.

How can I bring hope to my most trying relationship?

23

God, grant me the serenity to accept the people I cannot change, the courage to change the one I can, and the wisdom to know that one is me.

—ADULT CHILDREN OF ALCOHOLICS (ACA)
VERSION OF THE SERENITY PRAYER

Many of us have found ourselves tempted to try to change other people. "If only this other person would behave differently, then everything in my life would be easier!" we think exasperatedly to ourselves. While this idea of changing others is alluring, we learn through experience that it is ultimately frustrating and fruitless. There is so much in this beautiful and broken world that we cannot change. Other people are one of them.

This doesn't mean that we have no control. But in the course of recovery, we come to learn that our control has edges and limits, that there are some things we can change and others we cannot. As we begin to refocus on ourselves, we ask the Higher Power of our understanding to grant us courage so that we may take responsibility for our own actions and take care of our side of the street. We open our minds and our hearts to the healing process, humbly reaching out to others on this journey, asking for help when we need it, trusting that wisdom will grow inside us with time.

———————

Who do I find myself wanting to change today?
How can I redirect that energy back to my own life
in my thoughts and in my actions?

Maybe prayer doesn't mean talking to God at all.
Maybe it means just listening.

—Rev. Gary Kowalski

While writing this passage, I was in a time of needing help. My sponsor had asked me to reach out to people in my program, to make phone calls to strangers and ask for their help. This was terrifying. And it required me to keep an open mind. I was reaching out to people with a question and was instructed to just listen.

Listening with an open mind is not always easy for me. I often have a voice going inside of my head, telling me that I know better or have had a different experience. To just listen with an open mind and heart requires me to quiet that voice, to just receive the gift of another person's experience.

In the first call I made, I heard some extremely helpful advice and was given actions to take that were also helpful. The person was willing to offer help, and they did so in such a gracious way. It made the rest of the calls flow smoothly. By the time I hung up after the last conversation of the day, I realized that the voice that gets in the way of my listening had disappeared. Embracing an open mind and fully listening to another person was exactly what I needed to get out of my own head. What a gift!

———————

Where might I find an opportunity to listen to
someone else with an open mind and an open heart?

25

Praise the path on which we're led.
Praise the roads on earth and water.
Praise the rain; it brings more rain.

—JOY HARJO

As we begin the journey of recovery, it is so easy to focus entirely upon what we have done and upon what we will do. We reflect deeply on the choices we have made in our past that have led us to this place, and we wonder with hope-filled hearts about the future that awaits us as we continue to heal. But in all of these memories and daydreams, we often lose sight of the one thing that is truly ours—this singular, present moment. And while it is often challenging, there is much to be grateful for in the present. For in this moment, we have our recovery. For in this moment, we have beginnings and endings, music and rain.

On this day, we choose to move through the world from a place of gratitude, gratitude for another day to be alive and to be involved in the work of healing. Today will not be perfect. No day ever is. Today may even be difficult in many different ways. And we must acknowledge these challenges, while also recognizing that today will be full of small, sometimes imperceptible, gifts. We do our best to express our thanks for this beauty amid the brokenness. Today we open up our weary and courageous hearts and try to choose gratitude as an act of love and resistance.

What are the small (and large) things
that I am grateful for today?

But I challenge you; I charge you: if here is where you're tuned out, this is precisely and exactly the time to tune in.

—Brittany Packnett Cunningham

I've always loved the words of Rev. Mark Morrison-Reed, included in our Unitarian Universalist songbook *Singing the Living Tradition*, that remind us that "the religious community is essential, for alone our vision is too narrow to see all that must be seen."

But any of us can get stuck, even when other people are around. I've been known to look only for people who think just like me, or for those who don't but who won't challenge me to expand my thinking.

Consultant Thomas Bandy has written a book for church leaders called *Kicking Habits: Welcome Relief for Addicted Churches*. Just as individuals struggle, systems can get stuck in destructive patterns.

In our work to dismantle systems of oppression, it may be easy to believe that engaging people who believe differently is not my work to do or not the work of the religious community. I want to open up to the charge, to the challenge of tuning in.

Where in my faith might I open my mind to a new challenge?

27

Affirming that hope, publicly expressed, energizes and enables us to move forward. Together we pledge action to transcend barriers—be they racial, political, economic, social, or religious. We pledge to make our tomorrows become our todays.

—LORETTA F. WILLIAMS

There is deep hope in the midst of the hopelessness of addiction. It seems counterintuitive, doesn't it? But there is hope. And the hope is found in the many stories of the folks who have survived, who are no longer using, and who are living fuller lives today than they ever could have lived before.

Hope can be found in a Higher Power—in something that is more important than I am. And that is an open definition, open to all who would seek to recover. How very Unitarian Universalist! Each of us is invited to define a Higher Power for ourselves, one that transcends the barriers we have placed, one that we can personally relate to and engage with.

And the hope is found in the action of our various recovery programs. Recovery is not for people who need it, it is for people who work it. There is a spiritual toolkit laid at our feet in recovery. It is our choice whether or not we are going to pick up that spiritual toolkit and begin using it to finally be free from the vicious cycle of addiction, one day at a time.

What is one thing I am hopeful about today?

*Came to believe in a power greater than ourselves
that could restore us to sanity.*

—Step Two

The first three words of this Step are so important to Unitarian Universalists. "Came to believe" honors that we are on a spiritual journey, one that can lead us to beliefs both expected and unexpected. We can view this Step as an openness to the faith journeys we are on, a listening to where we are being called, an embracing of a belief that might be different from the one we started with, and a recognition that spirituality is fluid, shaped by our experiences and backgrounds.

We come to believe in something that is going to guide us through recovery. We come to believe in a power that can get us out of the mess we have been in while struggling with addiction. We come to believe that that power can do for us what we could not do for ourselves.

By taking this Step, we are not saying we have arrived at some place of deep theological understanding. We are certainly not saying that we have reached an end point. We are saying that we have come to believe. And we can come to different beliefs as time progresses.

———

*What have I come to believe today that is different
from what I have believed before?*

29

We do not hold to a hope that is only attained in the sweet by and by. We hold that this world, this life, these bodies are the dwelling place of the sacred.

—REV. REBECCA PARKER

Unitarian Universalists find our hope in this world, in this time, in these bodies, in this community. The hope of recovery is a this-worldly hope as well. It is the belief that our bodies are sacred and worthy of our care. It is the belief in the power of healing that can take place. This is not an out-side-of-here hope. It is grounded in lived experience and in seeing the sacred nature of everyday life.

If we have been to a recovery group, we often hear during the welcoming words that these are spiritual pro-grams. In the spiritual, the hope of recovery and healing is born. We see it in the lives of those around us, in the stories of people who have been sober for decades. This is possible for us too, if we are willing to follow a spiritual path, a hope-ful path.

Our recovery relies on our being open to new possibili-ties. Our recovery relies on our recognizing the sacred all around us. Our recovery relies on regular spiritual practices that build mindfulness and connection. Our recovery relies on our embracing a larger hope in the present day.

What do I have to be hopeful about today?

March

STEP THREE: SURRENDER

Made a decision to turn our will
and our lives over to the care of
God, as we understood God.

1

Once the soul awakens, the search begins and you can never go back. From then on, you are inflamed with a special longing that will never again let you linger in the lowlands of complacency and partial fulfillment.

—JOHN O'DONAHUE

I remember when I was still in the disease of addiction and not wanting to get better. Everything seemed so carefree. I was just floating from one moment to the next, remaining continually numb under the influence of my substance of choice. It wasn't until I got sober that I realized what a mess my life had become. My life was unmanageable in so many ways, from finances to relationships and even my spiritual life. Getting sober was a real awakening to all that had been happening, everything I had remained blissfully unaware of.

And then reality set in, as sobriety continued. I learned about all the things I need to do to stay sober: be in community with people, continually own up to the ways I have wronged people, make amends where I can. No wonder I had stayed blissfully unaware! Continued sobriety is hard work.

But I would not trade it in for anything. In those moments when I was in active addiction, I was not living. I was truly miserable. Sure, the work of recovery is tough. And the work of recovery and sobriety is so rich and rewarding. My life is so much better now.

When have I been called to be truly, fully myself?

I did not want to die, but desperately wanted to be anywhere but there.

—ELAINE PAGELS

There's a prayer used in many Twelve-Step programs, inspired by words of the early twentieth-century theologian Reinhold Niebuhr:

God grant me the serenity
to accept the things I cannot change,
courage to change the things I can,
and wisdom to know the difference.

I used to think this prayer was trite, or clichéd—until I began to actually engage in real recovery work. It's easily memorized and therefore lets me have a portable tool to deal with things as personally sorrowful as the death of a child or as trivial as a flat tire.

In her book *Why Religion?*, Elaine Pagels writes, "We found no meaning in our son's death, or in the deaths of countless others. The most we could hope was that we might be able to *create* meaning." In this passage she copes better with her child's death than I used to cope with a flat tire. Maybe I felt that, because the flat tire was such a small concern, I could muster power over it. I was wrong. The Serenity Prayer, or even a simple sigh, can remind me to let go of the need to control even small things.

———

What thing, small or large, can I give up control over?

The moment of surrender is not when life is over, it's when it begins.

—MARIANNE WILLIAMSON

In April of 2005, by a grace I don't think I will ever truly understand, I surrendered to the truth of my life: that I am powerless over alcohol and my life had become unmanageable. I surrendered because I couldn't control when I drank or how much I drank. Drinking, thinking about my next drink, and trying to outrun my hangover were the most important parts of my day. More important than my family and friends—more important than my work—more important than my self-worth and my dignity.

Admitting that I was powerless was an act of surrender, and it was the moment of my liberation. I was always taught to never give in, to never give up, to never, ever surrender to anyone or anything. What I have come to know in recovery is that surrendering to the truth of my addiction has been the most empowering act of my life.

Am I able to find a moment in time when surrendering was a new beginning?

But in order for the person to really know what you're talking about—deeply, fully—she or he will have to experience it directly. So it is with the spiritual journey. No words can truly describe it; you must experience it for yourself.

—REV. ERIK WALKER WIKSTROM

They invited me to try getting down on my knees to pray. I thought, "What? I would *never* do that!" I had been struggling for years with an addiction, compulsive overeating, and couldn't stop. This was the first time I had worked with a sponsor in my program, and I'd never thought I'd get an ask like this.

But I was desperate. And I wanted to finally be rid of my addiction. I was tired of the daily cycle of swearing off certain foods and finding myself eating them by the early afternoon.

The next morning rolled around, and I decided I'd give it a go and try praying on my knees. It was awkward getting down there. I felt strange and a little scared. But once I began saying the prayer, a calm came over me. It was a calm that I had been seeking in this program—some deep inner knowing that all was going to be all right.

Getting back up was pretty awkward too. And I remember that something felt different. Hard to say what it was, but something had shifted for me. It felt good enough to try again, and so I did. The next time, I felt much less awkward. I am so grateful I was willing to give this practice a try.

What's something new that I am willing to try, just for today?

5

The system is broken. It's going to take the young people to fix it this time. We need new ideas, new life.

—PRINCE

The artist Prince said these words in a music video for his song "Baltimore," written after the death of Freddie Gray at the hands of Baltimore police. He was also inspired to cover the spiritual "Mary, Don't You Weep" in response to the deaths of thousands of young people due to gun violence.

In the Third Step, we "made a decision to turn our will and our lives over to the care of God as we understand God." I'm finding my version of God in the beauty of the music and in siding with those who work to bring more justice into the world. That's me turning my life over to what is good. It's me noticing that my will doesn't change things but that working with something larger (like music, like a living tradition, like old words reinvented) can provide a form of guidance.

Do I have something to which I can turn over my will and my life?

Be who God meant you to be and you will set the world on fire.

—SAINT CATHERINE OF SIENA

Years before I was able to admit that I am an alcoholic, I sought out my father for advice. After I laid out the situation and what I wanted to happen, my dad paused and said, "However it turns out, I hope it is, in the end, what's best for you."

Needless to say, his words didn't land softly. Of course, I knew how it should turn out. Who better to know what was the best thing to happen for me than me? The wisdom of his response has grown on me with and through sobriety. My dad taught me to act on the things that I can, and yet also to have the courage to know that the outcome is beyond my power to control.

Sobriety teaches me that there is a grace in surrendering to the limits of my own knowledge, in yielding to the boundary of my individual will. When we are able to surrender, to let go of the illusion that we have the ability to power through and fix every problem, we gain the space we need to ask for help, to accept life on life's terms, and to be open to the feelings we must feel in order to keep healing.

———————

Might I open myself to who I am to be?

If there is no struggle, there is no progress.
—FREDERICK DOUGLASS

One of the joys of engaging in covenanted community is the opportunity to keep on growing together. The Third Principle of Unitarian Universalism is "acceptance of one another and encouragement to spiritual growth in our congregations."

For example, I can practice surrendering as I continue my commitment to antiracism. I don't know the outcome of my efforts, but I can work on becoming okay with not knowing. I practice surrendering when I acknowledge that the work won't be finished in my timeline, and that I am not the expert but always a learner. I can pay attention to defensiveness when someone points out something that I need to change, and work on changing it.

I can also surrender in my relationship with my recovery group, where we don't always agree with each other, especially on outside issues. I can surrender as an act of letting go of self-will, trusting in a Higher Power that accompanies me. There is struggle in all of these areas of my life, but by committing myself to my recovery, in being part of the work of liberation, I am making progress.

———

What can I learn about my own behavior?
How might I find hope?

Change will not come if we wait for some other person, or if we wait for some other time. We are the ones we've been waiting for. We are the change that we seek.

—BARACK OBAMA

As folks living with addiction, we know something has to change. Each day begins with a new resolve to give up this substance that has hold of our lives. And each day that we again pick up that substance brings another moment of disappointment. This is not something we can swear off. There are no magic words to get us to stop. To be able to stop, we have to experience a full life change.

If we are honest with ourselves, we have been living a life where we want things to happen on our terms. We have tried to make those around us bend to our will. We have tried to force things. We have made resolutions—often without success. Often to our great frustration. Often to our detriment, to the point where life is too much to handle and we are back in our addictions again.

What needs to change is inside of us. We need to change in our foundations. Our perspective on life needs a drastic change. And we need help—if we could have brought about this change on our own, we would have done it already. We need help from others who have gone before us and help from something greater than ourselves to get sober and stay sober.

Who can I ask to help me along this journey to recovery?

You cannot find peace by avoiding life.
—MICHAEL CUNNINGHAM

In August of 2000, I made the acquaintance of the most adorable four-week-old yellow lab puppy. When she was all of eight weeks old, that little ball of fur and love became my dog, and I her human. We agreed to be each other's keeper—that we would tend to each other's spirit.

Bartlett loved anything that was round and bounced and needed to be brought back to me. When she was younger and her joints weren't an issue, she loved to run. Much to my delight and betterment, she loved me.

Twelve and a half years later, I needed to make the decision to let her go. I knew what had to happen—but although I surrendered to the inevitability of the moment, I was not entirely at peace with the decision.

Surrender is not necessarily about finding immediate peace, but about finding a pathway to peace. I knew intellectually that letting Bartlett go was kind and unconditionally loving—it was her time, and it was up to me to let her meet death with grace and dignity. So I did.

Surrender isn't about being passive. Surrender is about yielding to the limits of our own knowledge, our own abilities, and our own willpower. No matter how smart—how clever—how engaged we are, we are still only humans in need of others. In need of the grace to let go.

What does the word "surrender" mean to me?

*It's funny how some distance makes everything
  seem small,
And the fears that once controlled me can't get
  to me at all.*

—"Let It Go," from *Frozen*

I think often of the suggestion of family systems theorists to take the "balcony view," a wide-angle view from above that lets us take in the whole situation. We need to find some distance to make things seem small, especially all of the differences and small conflicts that can sometimes seem large in a church community.

Not engaging in negative behavior, not being attached to substances, but finding spiritual practices like meditation, walking, or deep breathing can give just the right amount of distance to let us determine how to handle something that used to baffle us.

"Let it go" is not the same thing as "blow it off." Letting things go is a way to gain perspective, a way to not let fear control us.

———

Is there something haunting me that I can let go?

11

Let the current
hold you,
let the current
guide you;
the river that gently flows
through your soul,
whispers:
"Come, let us worship."

—REV. MANISH K. MISHRA-MARZETTI

When we are finally done fighting. When we are tired and worn out. When we have tried our various plans and designs and they have not worked. When we have been clinging to control with white knuckles, believing that this time, this time, *this time* it will all work out as we want it to. When it doesn't work out that way, and we try the same strategies over and over again.

Who are we to hold this tight grip? What would it look like to let go?

It looks like giving up the fight. It looks like accepting our tiredness and reaching out for help. It looks like releasing our plans and designs and going with the flow. It looks like listening to those who have gone before us. It looks like living life open and unguarded. It looks like open palms, inviting a great current to guide us one day, one moment at a time.

Where can I loosen my grip on control today?

Baseball is like church. Many attend,
but few understand.

—LEO ERNEST DUROCHER

Many years ago the place where I worked was part of a softball league. Of all the games we stumbled our way through, there was one in particular that still stands out for me.

We were playing a make-up game against a particularly dreaded opponent. Because it was a make-up we didn't have a real field scheduled, so we had to play in the middle of a city park. We had to supply our own bases and mark off where they should all be.

As the game wore on so did our nerves, because the bases weren't set into the ground and they would slip every time anyone tried to step on one.

In one particularly important play toward the end of the game, one of our opponent's players rounded first and was heading for second, only to get thrown out because he couldn't find the base in time. Well, all heck broke loose in a great and blustery argument.

Our shortstop managed to break through the noise and said as loudly as he could, "Second base may not be where you think it should be, but it certainly is where it is!"

Whenever I am faced with a situation that is not what I want—not what I can control—yet what I must accept, I say to myself, "Second base may not be where you think it should be, but it certainly is where it is!"

———

How can I extend acceptance to where I am today?

13

The hand that you hold belongs to a person who is seeking wholeness, and trusts that you're doing the same.

—REV. ERIKA HEWITT

I've heard it said many times in the rooms of recovery that "you're right where you're supposed to be." It takes a level of trust to listen to that voice and actually hear that lesson. Sometimes, in my Unitarian Universalist faith, it's easier to have doubt than it is to believe, or trust, or realize that things take longer than we might expect them to.

On a day when nothing but good happens, I am able to feel that all is happening at the right pace. When things don't go the way I want, I struggle. But as we fight the sense of urgency that permeates our culture, we are actually able to move toward wholeness.

What am I fighting against that doesn't allow me to trust the process?

*trust the people to do everything better than you
could have imagined.
trust the people and they become trustworthy.*

—ADRIENNE MAREE BROWN

Day after day, moment after moment, the word keeps coming to me: "Trust."

Trust is in the moments when I forget just how small I am. It is in the moments when I am asked to rely on human community for help. Trust is in the relationships I build with those in my community I am learning beside, and especially those who have something to teach me. Trust in people. Trust in God.

I struggle sometimes, because I was raised in a home where addiction was present. So much felt unpredictable and unreliable. Who was going to show up today? What was going to happen? Some days were smooth as silk. Others thorny as rosebushes.

But the message keeps coming, so I do my best to listen and to act accordingly. Recognizing that trust builds slowly for me, and that is okay.

Where do I experience trust?

15

Judge a tree from its fruit, not from its leaves.
—EURIPIDES

Several years ago, when I was just starting to learn how to lift weights, I summoned the courage to venture up to the main weightlifting floor of my gym. Early on in my venture, when I had the large room pretty much to myself, in walked the biggest—and scariest—weightlifter I had ever seen. He lifted only huge amounts of weight and didn't seem remotely friendly.

Each time I saw him, the story I imagined of who he was grew. Then one day our paths actually crossed when we both headed for the same machine. Before I could speak or react in any way, he stopped and in the softest, sweetest voice he apologized for stepping in my way and said, "Please, go ahead." All of a sudden, the big, mean person I had made him out to be was gone—and the person he truly was was right in front of me.

It is not an entirely comfortable place to be when I find myself butting up against my own judgments, and yet that place is so profoundly enlightening. Those moments are a reminder that no matter how hard I try to put people in tidy categories, they just won't stay there. We humans are too complex—too layered—too unpredictable to be boxed up or in.

---

*Where today might I surrender my judgments
to open myself to complexity?*

I have been driven many times upon my knees by the overwhelming conviction that I had nowhere else to go. My own wisdom and that of all about me seemed insufficient for that day.

—ABRAHAM LINCOLN

Most Unitarian Universalists I know do not like to spend time on their knees. As a young person, I was one of them, until I realized how my ability to surrender was a gift and a pathway to becoming a stronger human.

What did it mean to surrender? Who or what was I surrendering to? Rather than thinking of surrender as yielding to "the enemy," I needed to find a power greater than my own particular wisdom, so that surrendering felt like peace and acceptance instead of humiliation.

What I have found, over these years, is that getting on my knees puts me in a healthier relationship with the world, with the God of my understanding. I am not in a war with some evil adversary; my surrendering simply means that I am no longer fighting anything or anybody.

Whether my struggles are small or as important as those of a US president, getting on my knees brings me intelligence outside what I could previously have known.

Am I willing to get on my knees today?

17

*This path will ask much from us. Let us move forward
with love. Let us move forward with appreciation for
one another. Let us move forward knowing we are not
alone. Whoever you are, whatever your gifts, you are
welcome to join this journey.*

—REV. LYN COX

And then one day, it happened. Things began to feel lighter.
I felt a part of something larger. The heaviness didn't rest
solely on my shoulders.

I had been trying to control so much. To be all things to
all people. To make sure things happened the way I believed
they needed to happen. No wonder I was using. It was all so
overwhelming.

But it doesn't have to be that way. We are not meant to
control, to exert power over others, to make life bend to
our will. It doesn't have to be this way. There is a way out.
And the way out is surrender, is to embrace my own powerlessness, to recognize that I am one finite being in a world
of beings.

———————

What could surrender look like in my daily life?

*Let there be an opening
into the quiet that lies beneath the chaos,
where you find the peace you did not think possible
and see what shimmers within the storm.*

—JAN RICHARDSON

When I was drinking, my life was nothing but a storm. A storm that swirled around me as my life became more and more unmanageable with every drop. A storm that I was constantly trying to submerge on the inside with every drop I drank. I drank to numb myself, to try to outrun my feelings, who I was, what I wanted, what I needed. I drank to quell my fears and anxieties. I drank to keep the outside world away and my inner self hidden.

Admitting that I am powerless over alcohol meant that I was going to have to face the storm that I had so desperately tried to numb away. What I have found out is that living my all-too-human life is not always easy—but it is always easier than drinking. Recovery has given me the tools I need to face life on life's terms. Sobriety has given me a peace I "did not think possible" and allows me to "see what shimmers within the storm."

_____

*Might I find an opening amidst the chaos
to see what shimmers?*

19

Pray, and let God worry.
—MARTIN LUTHER

At the beginning I realized that if recovery was going to work long term, I had better find a way to pray. There are many more ways that prayer can work than are suggested in certain recovery programs.

Erik Walker Wikstrom, in his book *Simply Pray*, suggests using prayer beads, stringing or even making them oneself. I like that a Unitarian Universalist has written a whole book suggesting a serious spiritual practice to folx often averse to such things. He suggests that "old voices" come into our heads, and repetitive prayer is an antidote to that old way of thinking.

But this isn't the only way that prayer can work in my life today. I have recently begun an at-home long-term course in meditation, and the silence is a gift. I have no memorization, no beads, no particular chair, but I remember to stop, mid-day, and sit in silence for ten minutes. Amazingly, after that brief time, I am much more centered, more able to face the next half of the day.

I know people who have what they call a "God box." They write notes of their worries and place them in the box. Whatever they believe about God, they have simply set their worries aside. Chances are good that solutions to their problems are easier to find when they let the box do the work.

How can I pray today?

Believe in life! Always human beings will live and progress to greater, broader, and fuller life.

—W. E. B. Du Bois

When I first got sober, the thought of letting go of control was terrifying. What I didn't know until I stopped drinking and began to restore myself to sanity was how very little control I had over people, places, and things. Surrendering the illusion of control doesn't absolve me of the responsibility to act on the things I can change. Rather, it requires me to collaborate with what is best for me instead of resisting it.

If I stay in that unhealthy loop of trying to change things that are beyond my control, then I cannot grow, I will not continue to heal. When I do this I become my own version of Sisyphus, trying to wrangle the boulder of life up an unclimbable hill. What I need to focus on are the things I can change: the very few parts of my life and being I can control. The relief that comes with letting go opens a myriad of new, healthier possibilities that are waiting.

———————

How has acting on my own self-will affected my life? How has it affected others?

21

If you surrender completely to the moments as they pass, you live more richly those moments.
—ANNE MORROW LINDBERGH

If Anne Morrow Lindbergh were alive today, she would likely be talking to us about mindfulness. She would speak about the peace found through a regular practice of meditation, how a regular routine allows her to be in a place of peace.

In his book *Recovering Joy: A Mindful Life after Addiction*, Kevin Griffin discusses a breathing exercise from the Buddhist monk and author Thich Nhat Hanh that goes "In, Out; Deep, Slow; Calm, Ease; Smile, Release; Present Moment, Wonderful Moment."

Kevin is a Buddhist practitioner as well as a Twelve-Step adherent. As someone who meditated before recovering from addiction, he realized he needed not only meditation but also the practices and principles that addiction recovery forced him to see. Now, with them coupled together, his sobriety is ongoing, and his dharma writing is popular and authentic.

―――――――――

How might my daily work become more authentic through practicing a combined program of recovery and meditation?

May the sound of this bell penetrate deep into the cosmos
Even in the darkest spots
Living beings are able to hear it clearly
So that all suffering in them ceases
Understanding comes to their heart
And they transcend the path of sorrow and death.

—THICH NHAT HANH

Each day, I set a timer to remind me to say a prayer of surrender on the hour. This simple spiritual practice is often inconvenient—it happens sometimes when I am in work meetings or in the midst of grocery shopping. But isn't that what surrender is all about? It is not something that comes naturally to us. I would not need the help of my recovery program if my natural inclination was to surrender.

So, here I am, one hour at a time, trying on surrender. When the timer goes off, I stop what I'm doing for just a second and say a quick prayer or take a few deep breaths. When I fully embrace this practice, I can feel my shoulders relaxing from my ears back down to where they belong. I can take a moment to get out of the little plans and designs I've been holding in my head for the past few minutes.

Surrender is something I need to be consistently invited into and inconvenienced by. And when I embrace it, my day and my life flow so much better than they ever did before.

———————

How can I pause throughout this day and remind
myself to surrender?

*Silence is the language of god,
all else is poor translation.*

—RUMI

When I first came into AA, I let language keep me at a distance from the program and the people in the rooms. Step Three, "Made a decision to turn our will and our lives over to the care of God as we understood Him," was the most problematic of all the Steps for me. God? "Him"? "Higher Power"? The last thing I was ever going to do was to turn my life over to be rescued by a male authority figure.

As I worked the Steps—as I listened to others—as I listened to my own heart and spirit, I came to know that Step Three is not about submission to something that wants to control me. Rather, it is about surrendering my need to control. In the rooms when people are talking about Step Three they often say, "I don't know who my Higher Power is—all I know is it isn't me." Turning my will over, letting go of control, helps me to accept life on life's terms.

I've also realized that my wrestling with the language of Step Three was one of the ways my disease kept me from deepening my recovery. I'm still not sure who the God of my understanding is: Good Orderly Direction, Group Of Drunks, Grand Old Dyke. And I know that that doesn't matter as much as my knowing it's not me.

---

*Is my need to control other people's language
keeping me from living a full life?*

A Light exists in Spring
Not present on the Year
At any other period—
When March is scarcely here

— EMILY DICKINSON

I am so grateful to have spring in my life. What a time to begin something new, when buds are coming from the ground and appearing on trees. The season helps my recovery from addiction and my attachment to others' addiction by giving me a fresh offering of beauty and possibility. The metaphors are everywhere.

Yet the small buds and new grass also remind me that I am not fully ready for all things. Even though each day I wake there is something more to see and experience, I can't expect myself to be full grown when I am just a beginner.

What might the coming of spring teach me
about surrendering?

25

Every meditation I have ever done begins by asking me to ground myself. This is not so much an action as it is inaction. Surrender. A voluntary abandonment of my own edges and tidy packaging.

—JESS REYNOLDS

Surrender is about more than following instructions or doing what we are told we are supposed to do. The distinction is an important one. In submission or compliance, we are doing something to gain a benefit or some kind of reward. The motivating factor here is that if we don't do the thing, we may not get what we want or what we need. Compliance or submission is still a way to be in control, or at least to try to call the shots.

In surrender, the mind is clear, the posture is one of openness. Surrender is a way to seek guidance, to allow the shoulders to roll down from the ears, and to gently listen. In surrender, we join with something larger than ourselves. We concede we are not in charge. There is more at work in the universe than what is contained inside our own heads and hearts. May we breathe deeply today and choose surrender.

Where have I been compliant?
Where can I embrace surrender?

Literally, Wu Wei *means "without doing, causing, or making." But practically speaking it means without meddlesome, combative, or egotistical effort. It seems significant that the character* Wei *developed from the symbols for a clawing hand and a monkey, since the term* Wu Wei *means no going against the nature of things; no clever tampering; no Monkeying Around.*

—BENJAMIN HOFF

"Meddlesome, combative, or egotistical": a painfully accurate description of my will when I was drinking. I just didn't know it at the time. Step Three asks me to "turn my will over," to let go of the iron grip my will had on my life. Turning my will over simply means loosening my grip. If I'm worried or my fear isn't right-sized, then I'm more likely to tighten my grip. If I can lessen my grip and let go of what I can't control, then turning over becomes possible.

Can I get out of my own way to let this day unfold?

27

Jesus, take the wheel,
Take it from my hands
'Cause I can't do this on my own
I'm letting go

—BRETT JAMES, HILLARY LINDSEY,
AND GORDIE SAMPSON

"Jesus, Take the Wheel" was the first hit for country singer Carrie Underwood. And when I first heard it, I laughed, because I thought the lyrics were melodramatically ridiculous. But it's a good song, and now that I've listened to it many times over the years, it has become one of my favorites—a mantra for me when I'm going through a hard time.

It reminds me of "Precious Lord," believed to be Martin Luther King's favorite song. When life is hard, not only is it helpful to lean on something greater than ourselves, but also it's helpful to have words put to music.

I find it useful to put together a toolbox with as many implements as possible. And songs that remind me not only that I'm not alone but also that I need to let go, to surrender my false sense of control, actually help in healing.

———

What song helps me to remember to surrender?

Surrender is like a fish finding the current and going with it.

—MARK NEPO

I can remember a time when I was in a kayak on the water, and the current was extremely strong. Each time a dangerous obstacle loomed down the river, I got scared and began to paddle in all kinds of directions to get away from the tree stump or the rock I was certain I was set to crash into. Quite frankly, it was a toss-up as to whether or not I hit that stump or that rock. But the harder I fearfully fought, the more likely I was to sink or get caught.

And then there was my friend who consistently allowed the flow of the water to carry him. He would raise his paddle above his head and just float along with the current of the water. I looked at him in judgment at first and then in deep gratitude after he ditched his boat a few times to fish me out of the water.

I had so much to learn from him about what it meant to trust that the water would carry me. To learn how to go with the flow of the water rather than fearing it. To learn how to float rather than fearfully controlling.

Where has fear been guiding my actions? Are there ways for me to go with the current in a situation?

29

The past is always tense, the future perfect.
—ZADIE SMITH

Here's the kicker to Step Three: it's up to us—each of us—to decide to let go. We get to decide to do things differently, have a new outlook, trust the world and ourselves in a different way. We get to decide to become willing, or—as my sponsor likes to say—"willing to become willing."

When I was drinking, alcohol controlled every aspect of my life, was the deciding factor in all of my decisions. I moved through the world with one purpose—to drink—and everything was in service to that goal. Step Three is the foundation of reclaiming my ability to make my own decisions, to claim my own power, to commit my life to spiritual growth. All of this healthy empowerment is made possible by Step Three, which ironically begins with my surrender.

---

*In what way might I make surrendering
less of a scary ordeal?*

We are whole, even in the broken places, even where it hurts.

We are whole, even in the broken places, the places where fear impedes our full engagement with life; where self-doubt corrupts our self-love; where shame makes our faces hot and our souls cold.

—REV. BETH LEFEVER

Recovery has been a long journey toward self-acceptance. When we look at the process of accepting our powerlessness, getting right with ourselves, with a Higher Power, and with the people around us, it's possible that the last thing on our minds was to be accepting of ourselves. In seeking a spiritual solution, though, we are given both brief moments and long stretches of time of being at peace with ourselves.

There is nothing more we need to do to be worthy of love, to be worthy of the work of recovery. Whether we are still in the addiction or in the process of recovering from our addictions, we are whole and worthy of love. My Universalist ancestors knew this was so, and my Unitarian Universalist contemporaries know it too. We are loved for who we are.

So come, be at peace. Invite yourself into a moment of self-acceptance, even if just for the next thirty seconds. Repeat to yourself "I am whole. I am worthy of love" for a few rounds. See how you feel afterward. There's nothing else you need to do. You are loved.

Can I make time, just for today,
to remember I am loved?

31

For five thousand years, or more,
more than fifteen thousand generations,
human beings have been invoking spiritual power.
My predecessors, and yours,
have gathered together
to make sense of their lives
and their place in the cosmos.

—REV. MATTHEW JOHNSON

It is so helpful to know we are not alone and we are not here to reinvent the wheel. To embrace a Higher Power of our own understanding requires just one thing: that we believe in something more important than ourselves.

For some of us, this may be God or some form of deity. For others, it is human community. And for others still, it may be virtues like love, beauty, truth, and connection. For all of us, it needs to be something more important or bigger than we are. And it needs to be something we can access regularly for sustenance along our recovery journey.

There is hope in joining with the generations before us in seeking spiritual power. The hope is in the fact that we don't have to do this alone. And the hope is in the fact that connecting with a power greater than ourselves has worked for others—we see it in their lives and in their interactions. So come, hang on to the hope, and find that power that helps you to make sense of your life and your place is the cosmos.

Who has come before me in recovery from addiction
or even in my addiction lineage? Can I list out some
of their names and keep them with me for today?

April

Made a searching and fearless
moral inventory of ourselves.

The human body is robust. It can gather strength when it's in mortal danger.

—TONI MORRISON

We are beginning to understand that not only the family system we are born into but even the work we may do as adults in service of others and the world can bring with it a lot of trauma. The neurological nature of addiction protects us by revving up our brain to help us survive in a stressful situation, but that revving can give us the same addictive "high" that a drug can.

When we do a whole-life scan, we find that any number of factors—"people, places, and things"—can contribute to addiction. They could include the drama that always seems to occur with a family member, or on a shopping trip where I purchase more than I need or can afford, or with the rush that comes from working in the ER.

What are the people, places, and things to which I've made an unhealthy connection?

A mind is a system of ideas, each with the excitement it arouses, and with tendencies impulsive and inhibitive, which mutually check or reinforce one another.

—WILLIAM JAMES

It's pretty easy to make a list of people who have done me wrong, a little bit more difficult to make as long a list of those whom I have harmed. Supposing I blame the difficulty on my memory, why is making the first list so easy?

Imagining there may be a connection between the first and the second list, I will slow down, considering where I might have been partly responsible for the situation with the people with whom I am frustrated.

As I consider my complex system of ideas, I realize that I may have thought there was only one way to view a situation, and I may have gotten something out of that way of thinking.

―――――――

Can I pause to imagine what's upsetting me from another perspective?

3

We are here to face the truth, about ourselves, about the faith we love, and the ways it presently serves others and the world.

—Rev. Stephen Kendrick

To be able to honestly face the truth about ourselves in Step Four, we have to have a strong sense of faith. It is an act of trust to really look in the mirror and to get honest about who we are and what we have done. And it makes sense that we need a connection to something larger and more important than ourselves to hold us and guide us through this process.

Reliance on something larger than our individual selves gets built up in the Steps that come before. And to get into this place of surrender is a deep spiritual achievement. In surrender, we can trust that we will be carried through any difficulty—especially the difficulty of being honest with ourselves. Because true honesty is going to reveal things we would rather not see about ourselves, things we have been denying, and even things we were not previously aware of.

From this honest act, we can grow. Through being honest with ourselves, we know what we are working with. We can be in right relationship with ourselves. And from this foundation, we continue to take action so our recovery stretches out to getting into right relationship with the people around us and with a power greater than ourselves.

How does my faith or spiritual practice support me in being honest?

*The most common way people give up their power
is by thinking they don't have any.*

—ALICE WALKER

Addiction is such a complicated thing. Data shows that genetics play a big part, and the trauma that we experience as a child adds to the likelihood that we will develop an addiction.

As an adult, I have found that both therapy and an ongoing recovery program have helped me get some of my power back, especially by helping me see the power I already possess. They have helped me look at myself not with the hubris or inflated ego I had before recovery, but with a true sense of humility and self-love.

What power do I have today?

5

I will listen, and listen again, until my hearing becomes understanding.

—Rev. Erika Hewitt

When I first started going to meetings, I was just there to listen. I had no intention of sharing. I figured I'd listen for a few meetings, gather up all I needed, and head out of the rooms transformed.

It took another meeting or two of listening to people honestly sharing before I realized every person in there had a story similar to mine. I had gone into this thinking that I was unique in my experiences. But, alas, no. These were people who had been exactly where I was. And they were able to share freely and honestly about themselves. Sometimes, they even laughed about their experiences!

So I got up the courage to be honest with the group. I began telling my story and offering my perspective. And I began to get more out of being there. After a couple of months, someone approached me to let me know how much my honesty had meant to them. I was taken aback. I hadn't realized that what I had to say could be helpful to someone else in the way that others had been helpful to me.

All it takes is a room with a circle of people willing to be honest about their experiences to invite us to be honest about our own.

———————

What do I have to share today that would be helpful to someone else?

When you tell a lie, you steal someone's right to the truth.

—KHALED HOSSEINI

There are so many ways and reasons to lie. The reason may seem innocent. For instance, lying might be a way to preserve someone else's dignity. It's not that bad, and everyone does it, right? Many of us are taught to fib very well.

Some of us needed this survival skill to outlive childhood. Downplay the situation to keep our sanity or our safety. Cover up the indiscretions, ours or someone else's.

Whatever the reason, our integrity is not the only thing damaged when we are not truthful. It's not always about us.

There is another kind of falsehood. Prioritizing our intention over our impact is a form of dishonesty. When we do this, we steal someone's right to their truth, their experience. When we are honest with the fullness of a situation, when we listen to understand, then we can take responsibility. This is living honestly and with accountability.

Are there times when I am not completely honest? Besides myself, who else am I hurting? Who else has a right to the truth?

7

When you react, you let others control you.
When you respond, you are in control.

—BOHDI SANDERS

In *Daily Reflections*, a book by and for AA members, there is a reminder about the real problem of addiction. The anonymous writer reflects, "When I stopped drinking I began a lifetime process of recovery from unruly emotions, painful relationships, and unmanageable situations."

The reminder is that the substance or behavior of addiction is only a symptom of the problem, and the problem is that those who struggle with any form of addiction tend to be restless, irritable, and discontent.

There are so many tools to overcome addiction, like a daily spiritual practice and gathering together regularly with others who share their solutions.

———————

Where am I using my emotions in unhealthy ways?

Blessed are those brave enough to make things awkward, for they wake us up and move us forward.
—GLENNON DOYLE

It takes bravery to tell the truth, especially in moments when it might make things awkward. Sometimes it feels easier to keep moving forward as if nothing is happening. But do we actually move forward when we don't tell the truth? Do we actually grow that way?

I am a recovering food addict, and there have been so many uncomfortable moments with others as I share the truth about what I can and cannot eat. For a time, I thought it was just best to keep quiet. Food is such a sensitive subject, and I did not want to be a burden to anyone. But this only caused more unintentionally awkward moments, when folks found out they had prepared food for me I could not eat or when I just swallowed my truth and ate things that triggered my addiction all over again.

Healing from addiction has taken a lot of honesty and many awkward moments. It has taken times of really advocating for myself and for my recovery. Honesty is what I need to survive and thrive and live the most open-hearted, unguarded life I am able to live.

Are there spaces in the day ahead where I can tell the truth, even if it might be uncomfortable? Are there times in recent memory where I have not told the truth to avoid an awkward situation?

APRIL

9

There is some good in the worst of us and some evil in the best of us. When we discover this, we are less prone to hate our enemies.

—REV. MARTIN LUTHER KING JR.

A part of Step Four is to make a list of all of the people we have resented over the course of our lives, or even just in the immediate past. This is an honest part of recovery—a time to just get it all out in the open, to face what we have been feeling.

Each time I have made this list in my life, I have seen ways that the people I list have traits similar to my own. The things they do that I resent are often things I do to others that I am not proud of and even am often oblivious to. The people I have held resentments against thus become my teachers, folks I can learn about my shortcomings from.

It is amazing to me how complex human beings can be. Before this process of recovery, I thought of folks as good *or* bad, people I loved *or* people I resented. One of the gifts of this recovery process has been being able to see folks as all of these—to see the good, the bad, the loving, and the indifferent ways we all carry inside of us. We are more alike than I would have admitted before.

---

*What do I have in common with someone
I don't like right now?*

*Rarely have we seen a person fail who has thoroughly
followed our path. Those who do not recover are
people who cannot or will not completely give
themselves to this simple program, usually men and
women who are constitutionally incapable of being
honest with themselves.*

> —*ALCOHOLICS ANONYMOUS*,
> "THE BIG BOOK"

Search your heart. Is there something you are not willing
to be honest about? I imagine there is. There may be a few
things. Sometimes, we are dishonest because it is the kind
thing to do. Oftentimes, we are dishonest to save our own
skin—to make ourselves look good, to rationalize our behavior, and to reinforce old patterns we fear to break.

Search your heart. Is there something in there you are
not willing to be honest about? Perhaps a secret you have
been holding on to for a lifetime, or just since last week.
The things we cannot and will not be honest about often
lead us to compulsive behaviors, to addiction.

Search your heart. Are you willing to be honest now? Are
you able to find a way to be honest, even if only with yourself? This is the path toward putting the behaviors down and
beginning on a different path. You are capable of being honest. You have already begun.

---

*Is there something in my heart I am not willing
to be honest about?*

We think back to the friends we have made,
The sorrow we have endured
The love we have found
The loneliness we have survived.

—Rev. Mark Stringer

To tell our life's story from a place of honesty can be difficult. We have experienced heartbreak, times when we have fallen short of who we would have liked to be, and times of deep joy. If we have grown up in a family that lived with addiction, our life's story may be especially painful to tell. All the grief, all the control, all the desires to make it right.

My religious tradition invites me to embrace my imperfections. My Universalist ancestors would tell me, and all of us, that we are loved for who we are. As human beings, we often struggle to live into this. And it is good to know that our stories have shaped who we are, but they are not the final word on our core identity. Our stories need to be told, so we can honestly face where we have been our best selves and where we have not, remembering always that our life has been a mix of both.

So tell your story. And tell it honestly. Be real. Be willing to face where you have been and what you have come from. It is a healing experience and one you will not regret.

———

What part of my life's story is crying out
to be told today?

*Constantly take inventory of what's
important to you.*

—DAVE CHAPPELLE

Part of the suggested work of recovery is to make a "searching and fearless moral inventory of ourselves." There are our stated values, and then there are our acted-out values. If I look at my behavior, I can see what really matters to me. So how does my behavior reveal to whom I show love, who makes me angry, and where I spend my time?

I used to not be present to my surroundings, because of my use of a substance or behavior. Making a commitment to recovery began to show me how that kind of use was toxic to those around me and to myself.

These days, I still take a regular inventory. Bedtime is a good time to reflect on my day, what I could have done better, and whether I spent the day thinking of myself. At the end, I can ask forgiveness and sleep well.

As I arise, can I focus on the day ahead?

Spirit of truth, of life, of power, we bring ourselves as gifts to thee: oh, bind our hearts this sacred hour in faith and hope and charity.

—REV. HORACE WESTWOOD

In the church I serve, there are four human figures depicted in the four corners of the sanctuary, representing different virtues: Hope, Love, Faith, and Truth. Truth stands with one hand on their hip, staring straight ahead. The other hand holds a mirror up, reflecting back clearly whoever looks their way.

To look into that mirror as people who struggle with addiction can be so very hard. Sometimes the view gets fuzzy, clouded by the haze and the numbness of addiction. Other times, we look away, not wanting to see the ways our words and actions are hurtful to those around us that we love. And I know there have been moments when I have skewed my view of that mirror with justifications, lies, and deceit, just so I could keep on using the way I wanted to.

But Truth remains, soft-faced and continuing to hold the mirror, patiently awaiting the day when we are finally ready to face our stories and our histories. The clarity can be painful, but it is well worth it to be free of avoidance, dishonesty, and the cycle of addiction.

How can I look into a mirror of truth today?

To lie habitually, as a way of life, is to lose contact with the unconscious. It is like taking sleeping pills, which confer sleep but blot out dreaming. The unconscious wants truth. It ceases to speak to those who want something else more than truth. . . .

This is why the effort to speak honestly is so important. Lies are usually attempts to make everything simpler—for the liar—than it really is, or ought to be.

In lying to others we end up lying to ourselves. We deny the importance of an event, or a person, and thus deprive ourselves of a part of our lives. Or we use one piece of the past or present to screen out another. Thus we lose faith even with our own lives.

—ADRIENNE RICH

I finally had to take a break from social media. Especially Instagram. I couldn't take any more pictures of other people's supposedly perfect lives. I don't find my life that pretty or that apparently easy. I find life hard. And messy. When I spend a lot of time in other people's (or my own) illusions of life I disconnect from the beautiful, complicated awkwardness of real life. This is a form of dishonesty that isn't good for my health.

Where can I embrace my beautiful, complicated, hard, awkward real life?

15

A lack of transparency results in distrust and a deep sense of insecurity.

—The Dalai Lama

I have a friend who is a middle school counselor. She works at a school that I would have guessed to be fairly stable. But it seems that many of our schools, regardless of location, are filled with trauma. Children are tight-lipped about what's going on at home.

She has found that being transparent can be wise. Not that she tells them specifically of her struggles with addiction. But she shares enough that they can feel safe enough to open up, to see that the stories they have to tell are okay to share.

Our Twelve-Step programs are grounded in the principle of anonymity. It does not mean we are shame-based but rather that "we are to place principles before personalities; that we are actually to practice genuine humility." That doesn't mean that we can't be transparent about having overcome difficulties. It means that we can be honest with another when we might be helpful to that person. We can be honest when to do so will repair some past harm. We can be honest when to do so will give us a feeling of gratitude.

Where might I be withholding rather than being transparent?

Will you strike yourself
  against life's hard surfaces
  and let the flame out,
  or let it be born from your giving,
  let it be eternally released

to spread the light?

—Rev. Stephen M. Shick

You can recover.

You, whose life has been ravaged by addiction. You, whose loved one has gone back to the drink over and over again. You, who swore you would not pick up and then picked back up again. You, who are fresh from a treatment program. You, who have long been sober and went back for one last time. You, who have struggled.

You—yes, you—can recover.

You can recover because so many with your struggles out here have recovered. So many have joined together to share their experiences, ask for help, and begin working a program. So many have taken it painful day by painful day until the addiction is no longer both the source of and the treatment for the pain. So many have made the phone call instead of continuing in this isolating cycle alone.

We—yes, we—can recover.

Where have I struggled to believe I can recover?

Lying is, almost by definition, a refusal to cooperate with others. It condenses a lack of trust and trustworthiness into a single act. It is both a failure of understanding and an unwillingness to be understood. To lie is to recoil from relationship.

—SAM HARRIS

Unitarian Universalists center covenant, a holy agreement as to how we will journey together in relationship, in our communities. Sometimes explicit, sometimes implicit in those agreements is honesty. Honesty is required for mutuality. When someone cannot be honest, it is good and healthy to articulate consequences and boundaries.

When I was a young adult, I went through a period of being what I can only describe as a red-hot mess. I was undermining leadership, which is a refusal of cooperation and a form of lying. Bob, our church curmudgeon, took me for coffee and said, "To be blunt, your words and your actions aren't lining up. I need you to do better, because our community needs you. How can I help get you back on track?" That right there was love showing up. Awkwardly, mind you, but also faithfully and courageously. Well, Bob loved me into more aligned behavior. He got me back into right relationship.

―――――――――

How can I live into right relationship with trust and honesty by paying attention to my own behavior and by having courageous conversations with those who might be struggling?

Once I am identified with a story in which I assigned myself the role of victim, I don't want it to end, and so, as every therapist knows, the ego does not want an end to its "problems" because they are part of its identity. If no one will listen to my sad story, I can tell it to myself in my head, over and over, and feel sorry for myself, and so have an identity as someone who is being treated unfairly by life or other people, fate or God. It gives definition to my self-image, makes me into someone, and that is all that matters to the ego.

—ECKHART TOLLE

I think casting myself in the role of victim has been a problem since I was a little kid. When I was in second grade, my parents threw a party for me, and I was able to invite all my friends. It was a hit. Everybody had a good time. Except me. They took a black-and-white photo of us all lined up outside on our back deck. So I remember seeing that photo of everyone else's smiles and my scowling face, year after year, the rest of the family chuckling about it. Except me.

Today, rather than feeling bad that I missed an opportunity for fun, I can remember to let go of that self-pity and enjoy the day that faces me. Nobody wants to listen to the sad story, unless you're paying them, and even your therapist will suggest leaving behind this ego identity.

Today I can tell a new story.

———————

When I hear myself tell a sad story, even in my head, can I stop and change the story?

19

A sudden bird
speaks for us all,
each of us in solitary
solidarity, our lives unspoken,
already known to each other.

—REV. KAREN LEWIS FOLEY

I kept so many secrets.

Some seemingly big. Others felt smaller. Growing up in a house where addiction was all around us, I learned to keep my secrets guarded. I learned to put a smiling, happy face over the pain. I learned to speak with no one about the difficulties I was experiencing.

So the first time I walked into a recovery meeting and heard people speaking openly about a loved one's alcoholism or the home life they grew up in, the space seemed really scary to me. When I finally got up enough courage to give voice to my own story and struggles, it felt awkward at first. I was out of practice in telling the truths of my experiences.

It didn't get easier at first. In fact, telling the truth became harder the deeper I was willing to go. But, gratefully, I kept at it and I kept telling my truth with others who knew what I was experiencing. And slowly, eventually, telling the truth became easier and even became more desirable than keeping secrets.

What secrets am I holding on to that I could
talk about with a trusted friend?

Women have been driven mad, "gaslighted," for centuries by the refutation of our experience and our instincts in a culture which validates only male experience. The truth of our bodies and our minds has been mystified to us. We therefore have a primary obligation to each other: not to undermine each other's sense of reality for the sake of expediency; not to gaslight each other.

Women have often felt insane when cleaving to the truth of our experience. Our future depends on the sanity of each of us, and we have a profound stake, beyond the personal, in the project of describing our reality as candidly and fully as we can to each other. . . .

When a woman tells the truth she is creating the possibility for more truth around her.

—ADRIENNE RICH

Any person from a marginalized identity has experienced gaslighting. It is essential that we acknowledge as valid the experience of those most vulnerable. This is love. This is covenantal.

Being real with each other and holding each other's experience as sacred can be a transformational act of defiance, resilience, and solidarity.

Can I make a date with someone to share pieces of my life and be as real as I bravely can?

21

Come my truth,
a truth that has no loopholes
or moth-holes, or frayed edges.
A truth as exciting as fire, and as bright—
as powerful as water, and as fluid—
as solid as earth, but as transparent as air.

—Rev. Mark Belletini

I must admit, I love cake. I love to imagine it, to glorify it, to consider its ritual significance over time immemorial. I love to cut it, and I love to take a big bite, one with half cake and half frosting.

But as I was struggling with some health issues, my medical provider suggested I eliminate sugar from my diet. Not only is that hard to do—I mean, everybody these days knows how much sugar there is in ketchup—but I came to realize in that moment that I really, *really* love cake.

Truth is, I am addicted to sugar. I realized it when the thought of no more cake actually brought on a sense of despair. But admitting this, and using the tools of the Steps, can offer a solution. So, just for today, I don't need cake.

Is there something or someone I love
in an unhealthy way?

We think back to the times when we were afraid and uncertain and we trudged ahead anyway, and the times when we were compassionate when we could have been cold.

—REV. MARK STRINGER

It was so hard to be honest when I was in the midst of my addiction. I had a reason for everything. And there were so many opportunities to lie, whether to mask my behavior or so that I could just keep doing drugs.

And then came the moment when I ultimately had to be honest:

Am I addicted to these drugs?

The thought had crossed my mind before, and I had pushed it away or rationalized my behavior. This was just for fun, right? Sure, I was using every day, but I wasn't as bad as some of my friends. There were so many things I told myself to keep my thoughts away from the truth.

But the day came when I had to look hard at that question, and I found the answer was "Yes." And instead of all the bad feelings I thought I would be feeling, all the things I had been avoiding for so long, I felt relief. The sweet relief that comes when we can finally stop lying to ourselves and embrace our own truth.

When have I experienced relief and/or compassion in response to honesty?

23

So bring your brokenness, and I'll bring mine
'Cause love can heal what hurt divides
And mercy's waiting on the other side
If we're honest
If we're honest.

—FRANCESCA BATTISTELLI

The song starts out, "Truth is harder than a lie" and goes on, "I'm a mess and so are you. We've built walls nobody can get through. Yeah, it may be hard, but the best thing we could ever do, ever do."

People often build walls of lies in order to gain approval. But it's a false approval, false power. The paradox is that truth breaks down those walls and gains us deeper approval. When we declare, "I'm a mess and so are you," embracing that vulnerability, the relationship gets real.

That kind of honesty requires trust. How does one build trust? Experts suggest a number of ways:

- consistently showing up for another, doing what you say you're going to do
- being open to feedback, yet sincere in your reactions
- untangling yourself from triangulation and gossip
- embracing your own vulnerability
- taking responsibility when you mess up, changing your behavior, and then asking for forgiveness.

Trust takes practice. Consider it a spiritual practice.

Who are my friends with whom I can be a broken mess?

Most [people] would rather deny a hard truth than face it.

—GEORGE R. R. MARTIN

Honesty is a principle of recovery work because so often denial has been the operative force of an active addict's life. It wasn't until I began working with others newer in recovery from addiction that I began to really see my own hidden areas of truth.

Each day, I need to do some self-examination, with a sponsor and my Higher Power, to release the denial that still is so easy to cling to. Even now, when I understand it intellectually, it takes a while to see how I have harbored a resentment, or thought of myself more highly than I should.

All the steps we take can make our interior life more serene and move us toward healthier behavior.

Have I spoken to my sponsor lately about what's really going on?

25

By no means are we [Unitarian Universalists] perfect; we often fail as much as we succeed. Yet even when "we have broken our vows a thousand times," we return to this essential work of justice and liberation for all.

—REV. ROSEMARY BRAY MCNATT

In my Fourth Step, I was advised to write down on my resentments list anything that was bothering me, no matter how small. This invitation gave me space to write down systems of oppression like racism and misogyny and transphobia. These were certainly the driving forces behind laws, policies, and actions that harmed me and my friends.

My next step was to look at ways my resentments were keeping me from taking action to eradicate these systems. While remaining in resentment, I did not want to accept the realities of oppression, and I was spending precious energy on frustration rather than adding that energy to struggles for justice. My sponsor helped me to see ways my ego was involved—ways I wanted to have the appearance of doing the work rather than actually doing it.

This deeply impacted the justice work and commitments I hold. I am so grateful for the invitation to delve deeply into what I resent to get to the fears, the insecurities, and the dishonesty that are revealed as a part of the Fourth Step process.

Where are my resentments and image management getting in the way of my being an effective presence in movements for justice?

*Ego is not who we are, it's who we want people to
think we are, and, also, who we think we are.*

—RONNIE HERREMA

You've probably been in a conversation with someone who was leading with ego. It's more of a monologue, because ego isn't there to listen but to exert power over others and feed the false self.

Sometimes we collude with another person's ego. If we're uncomfortable being honest with someone, we are likely agreeing not with them but with their ego. We go along with it. Sometimes we get lazy or lulled into the familiarity of the lie, and it feels easier to just let honesty go. But then, are we in a real relationship with them?

Break the pattern by leading with loving honesty. It isn't easy. It can be scary and awkward. It takes practice. Spiritual practice.

Maybe you've been the person leading with ego, which can be lonely and exhausting and always unsatisfying. Living in honesty requires that we pay attention to when we are centering our ego, and once we recognize it, unplug from the false source of self and replug into our core self, which is love. Our real self isn't about ideas; it's about love. What brings you back to love? Go there. No need to beat yourself up. Just notice and get back to love.

---

*How can I break patterns within myself and with
others that I may disconnect from ego and other
false selves to reconnect to love?*

27

My desire to be honest with myself made it necessary for me to realize that my thinking was irrational.

—*ALCOHOLICS ANONYMOUS*,
"THE BIG BOOK"

Prior to recovery, I had no idea that honesty included my relationship with myself. I thought honesty was simply about my relationship with others or the cash register. As I approached Step Four, making a searching and fearless moral inventory, I was able to use the clarity I gained by taking Steps One, Two, and Three. Because I was no longer using the behavior of my addiction, I had also experienced the "psychic change" talked about in the "big book." These tools have allowed me to appreciate where I was kidding myself and how my spiritual capacity has increased through recovery.

When I look at the day ahead, rather than looking at it with a cloudy sense of dread because I'm covering something up, I can now face it with a feeling of joy. Even on a day that feels hard, I at least carry a sense of competency because I have tools to use. I keep striving for honesty because I know am better for it.

Might I use the trust gained in Step Three
as I make a searching and fearless
moral inventory of myself?

Cherish your doubts, for doubt is the servant of
truth. . . . Yet in our inner rooms full of doubt, inquiry
and suspicion, let a corner be reserved for trust. For
without trust there is no space for communities to
gather or for friendships to be forged.

—Rev. Michael A. Schuler

In this post-truth world, I think doubting is a skill we people of faith need to hone. Especially since we cherish and value honesty.

The first person I doubt is myself. I see doubting myself as a form of self-love on the path to honesty. People who know me well know that I have a lot of big feelings and am prone to hyperbole. When my partner and I first got together and were in that phase where you tell each other your life stories, she'd interrupt me mid-story and ask, "Is that true?" At first it seemed downright rude. Was she calling me a liar? No, she was giving me the gift of doubt.

Byron Katie calls this doubt The Work: Is this thought true? Can you absolutely know that it's true? How do you react when you believe that thought? Who would you be without the thought? Through this exercise of doubt, you gradually surrender, until you arrive at a pure honesty and self-trust.

How can I hold the doubt and the questioning of my
convictions until I arrive at wise honesty and
self-trust?

29

It is important to be honest about our complicated history, not to bring shame or guilt, but to bring understanding that can inform our faith today.

—Rev. Susan Frederick-Gray

I can compassionately trust that I did the best I could with what I had at the time and knew at the time. But honestly? Sometimes it wasn't enough, or it didn't quite hit the mark of my current values. I look back and am a little squeamish at things I did in my past.

Thank goodness no one will ever be possessed to write my biography, because I shudder to think what an author would make of the more, ahem, *complicated* parts of my life. Most of us have those. Some more than others.

Life doesn't have a rewind button. But our imaginations can conjure one to help make meaning of our complicated histories. I often ask myself, "If I had a rewind button, what would I do differently?" And the meaning that I derive from that exercise is what I will judge myself on. What have I learned from my complicated life that helps me live with more abundant honesty and integrity?

How can I affirm I am not my mistakes?
How can I affirm I am the culmination of my learning and new choices?

Clients don't expect perfection from the service providers they hire, but they do expect honesty and transparency. There is no better way to demonstrate this than by acknowledging when a mistake has been made and humbly apologizing for it.

—Patrick Lencioni

We live in a white supremacy culture: one that systematically denigrates, devalues, and harms people of color. The ways that white supremacy is manifested include many that, on their face, may seem to be unrelated to race. One of them is the expectation of perfection. White supremacy culture leads us to believe that it's reasonable to consistently expect perfection, and leads many of us to feel shame or guilt when we don't attain it. We may try to hide the evidence of our "failure." There are whole industries making profits on that illusion of perfection and the aftereffects of the inevitable failure to achieve it.

Here's the thing: no reasonable person is asking for perfection. What we need from each other is honesty. Honesty builds trust; perfection does not. Recognizing our mistakes, fixing our blunders, asking for forgiveness, and then beginning again are hallmarks of honestly and integrity.

When have I tried to attain perfection, failed, and then tried to hide my failure? How did that go? When have I made a mistake, acknowledged it, and humbly apologized for it? How did that go?

May

Admitted to God, to ourselves, and
to another human being the exact
nature of our wrongs.

1

If we are brave enough often enough, we will fall; this is the physics of vulnerability.

—BRENÉ BROWN

I remember the last time I fell. It was at the end of a perfect run, but I had pushed the run too hard and my legs were tired. My toe caught a rock in the trail and down I went. Hard. I was staying at a friend's place and didn't want people to make a big fuss about me, so I walked into the house nonchalantly and tried to pretend as if nothing had happened. Of course, the moment my friends saw me, they hauled out the rubbing alcohol and bandages and began tending to my injuries. I remember feeling so cared for as they wrapped my arm.

Those of us who are alcoholics know what it's like to fall down. When I first entered sober rooms, I wanted to prove that I didn't really have a drinking problem. I was smarter than that. I was guarded with the other people around me. Yet gradually, one day at a time, I began to open up to people who welcomed me. I began to share at meetings. It felt as if my own wounds had begun to heal.

Sobriety requires vulnerability. It also requires the courage to fall and to pick oneself up, to allow oneself to be tended to by others who themselves know what it's like to fall, and to get up and to heal. It is, as Brown reminds us, the physics of vulnerability.

How will I allow myself to be vulnerable today?

The church is a body.
It is as vulnerable as the most newborn and untried
of its members.
It is ancient, and it is ever new.

— REV. VICTORIA WEINSTEIN

It took a lot for me to reach out for help. Years of committing to ask for help to get sober tomorrow. Tomorrow I will give up that substance. Tomorrow I will be new. Tomorrow I'll call that person who offered to help me or to bring me to a meeting. Tomorrow, tomorrow, tomorrow.

Finally, a day came when the pain was too great. I had to reach out for help or else I would live a lifetime of waiting until tomorrow. I reached out to that person who had offered to help me months before, and the help was right there when I needed it.

We are always new when we are first reaching out for help. What matters is that we are reaching out. It is a vulnerable moment, but accepting the help of another person is a life-saving, life-giving act. Without help, I would not be alive today.

Who are two or three people I know I can rely on for help? What have they done to let me know they will help me? How can I be available to help others?

3

I became a writer out of desperation. . . . When I was young, younger than I am now, I started to write about my own life and I came to see that this act saved my life.

—JAMAICA KINCAID

Stunningly beautiful days take us outside or make room for a kind of peace at the window to write. Whether we use a three-ring notebook, a beautifully bound journal, an old-fashioned typewriter where striking the keys is a meditation practice in itself, or the convenience of a computer, writing can improve health. Louise DeSalvo, author of *Writing as a Way of Healing*, explains that one way of writing about trauma has been clinically shown to improve health. "We must write in a way that links detailed descriptions of what happened with feelings—then and now—about what happened."

That isn't necessarily an easy thing. (And DeSalvo warns us not to use writing as a substitute for physical or mental health care.) But taking twenty minutes a day to work on it, for a number of days every now and then, can be a beginning. Joys and pleasures can be part of the writing.

What is my story? Can I make space to be honest about my experiences?

God, grant me the courage to have a streak of steel when I need it, the courage to express my vulnerability when I need that, and the wisdom to know when to do which.

—REV. ROGER BERTSCHAUSEN

Those who have been in recovery have most likely encountered the Serenity Prayer, which begins, "God, grant me the serenity to accept the things I cannot change, the courage to change the things I can, and the wisdom to know the difference." While in the throes of addiction, we do all we can to manipulate people, places, and things so that we can continue to drink. We do this because we believe that alcohol will numb the pain of living. It can protect us against our own feelings of sadness, loss, grief, or disappointment.

Sometimes we do need a streak of steel in us to stand up to the ever-present temptation to drink. That "streak of steel" is made stronger by having relationships with others in recovery and working a program of recovery. Sometimes, we need the courage to express our vulnerability: to acknowledge that we can't do this alone and that, in fact, trying to soldier on through life on our own has made us vulnerable to the temptation to drink. To be in recovery is also to be discerning about what we need and to take responsibility for our needs.

What is the streak of steel that I can draw upon today to stay on the path of sobriety?

5

The willingness to show up changes us.
It makes us a little braver each time.

—BRENÉ BROWN

I believe in the power of community. Whether it's the one-on-one ministry of listening to another person in a covenant group, participating in Sunday worship, or singing with tens of thousands in the seventh-inning stretch of your favorite baseball team, being part of community is powerful.

Martin Buber describes the I/thou relationship as ultimately being with God, which requires vulnerability.

Ministry of presence is a "showing up" of sorts, whether we show up for another or are vulnerable enough to allow them to show up for us.

————

Can I express vulnerability by showing up for
another or allowing them to show up for me?

but here was one
who could take us into his personal life
and show us around
as if it were a house for sale
exposing everything the way it was

—RIC MASTEN

In order for us to recover from our addictions, we have to get honest. Really honest. And not just honest about whether or not we are addicted, though that is important. We have to get honest about our personal lives, about our fears, about the emotions and the stories that drive us to use. In being honest and then being vulnerable with another person about where we have made mistakes or come from a place centered in ego, we move toward surrender and trust.

We are also asked to be honest with another person— to lay it all out for them to see. In following this path, we discover we are not alone. We also hear a perspective outside of our heads. Most of the time, the people who are listening to us have been there too.

To risk vulnerability with someone else is to really allow them to see us. It is a risk in that someone will know us for who we truly are, a side of us we don't believe we show to the world. And the rewards are great: serenity, neutrality around our substances, and a different perspective.

Who do I know who lives a life in which everything
is honestly exposed, just as it is?

*The gift of grief is an affirmation of life,
and of our intimacy with the world.*

—Rev. Mark Belletini

To live is to lose; to lose is to grieve. All of our lives we are living and losing something. We may lose a grandparent, a sibling, or a parent. There are other losses, too, not visible to the outside world but that we feel deeply. We may lose confidence in our ability to navigate through the world, to be a productive human being. We may lose faith in our fellow human beings or in ourselves.

How, then, do we deal with the losses of life? As an alcoholic, I used to think that the natural response to loss and grief was to drink. It was as if drinking would somehow inoculate me against feeling grief. I also believed that my feelings of loss and grief were so uniquely deep that I had the *right* to drink them away.

The truth of the matter is that to live is to lose and to lose is to grieve. It's the human condition. What I learned in sobriety is that there is another way of handling grief and loss. Instead of running away from it to the false comfort of alcohol, I allow grief to sit beside me. By allowing myself to be vulnerable to these feelings, I also allow my companions, grief and loss, to watch over me.

Can I imagine my feelings of grief and loss as intimate companions? Can I allow them to just be, without feeling the need to push or drink them away?

Vulnerability is the birthplace of innovation, creativity, and change.

—BRENÉ BROWN

Social scientist Brené Brown finally brought vulnerability into the mainstream. She lifted it from a negative into a positive quality. We see it now as a virtue, an opportunity for personal spiritual growth and courageous social justice action.

But it's not just something you stick on like a temporary tattoo. It takes effort to move into this way of being, free from alcoholic or drug-induced behavior. It takes sustained sobriety and engaging with one day at a time.

As a child, I was taught that vulnerability was a negative quality. When I was vulnerable with people as a kid, the response was often being told I was "too much." I still wanted to be open as an adult, and for a while alcohol served as a false way to be vulnerable with others. Alcohol provided a temporary easing of the walls I had built up, but it was never about truly sharing my struggles with others. It was often a quick, drunken confession I regretted the next day.

Today, free of these past thoughts and behaviors, I am able to see vulnerability as a part of health and connection—true connection.

———

What do I need to look at before I can consider my own vulnerability?

My God asked me, Do you love yourself?
I said, Does it matter?
She said, YES!

—REV. MARK HICKS

I was talking with my sponsor, going over my Fifth Step, a time to review some of the resentments and fears I had been holding on to. As she patiently listened and helped me to go deeper, asking questions, offering her perspective, she began to notice a pattern. I was taking each of my shortcomings and using them to speak poorly about myself.

Growing up in an alcoholic home, I heard many messages at an early age about how I was not good enough. And whether they were spoken or just wordlessly communicated, I internalized them. Being not good enough became the foundation out of which I operated.

My sponsor asked me, "What do you think your Higher Power wants for you?" I took a moment to be quiet and to listen before responding. "I think my Higher Power wants what is best for me—for me to live a full, authentic, and honest life." And so the mirror was held up. A mirror I could have never looked into honestly without the help of another person. I am so grateful for her guidance that day.

What foundational story from times past am I
carrying around in my head today?

My grace is sufficient for you, for my power is made perfect in weakness.

—2 CORINTHIANS 12:9

The complex Biblical character known as Paul of Tarsus is someone that many alcoholics can relate to. If you met him in a bar you'd probably recognize something of yourself in him. He probably was the center of attention, talking loudly and fast, and drawing people to him with the charisma of his personality. He had big dreams and big ideas and could be heard boasting of his next big project.

And yet he had what he describes as "a thorn in his flesh," and three times he asked God to take this weakness away from him. He writes that God answered him by saying, "My grace is sufficient for you, for my power is made perfect in weakness." As alcoholics, we can feel that alcohol gives us a kind of power. But even though we may believe that drinking gives us power or at least a few moments of insight, we know that it also brings much worse things. We may feel that it's weak to ask for help—to seek recovery. Yet, strangely enough, it is in the moment when we surrender that we discover a different kind of power emerging. When we make ourselves vulnerable to recovery, our understanding of power and weakness is transformed. We begin to see that what we once thought of as a weakness is now made perfect in our sobriety.

What do I consider my greatest weakness? What is the source of my own personal power?

11

I long, as does every human being, to be at home wherever I find myself.

—MAYA ANGELOU

I used to feel uncomfortable with myself. I did not want to be the kid on the playground who stood alone by the fence. I wanted to be in the crowd with the popular vibe. As I got older, the feelings got stronger and became what these days they call FOMO, or "fear of missing out." I believe, at its core, that fear is a discomfort with oneself, the sense that the grass is greener or the people prettier or smarter somewhere else.

These days, I have tools to help me notice when the discomfort arises, to note when I am hungry, angry, lonely, or tired, and to be reminded that I am right where I am supposed to be. It takes vulnerability to admit my longings, yet an ongoing practice allows me to begin to be at home in (or at least be able to manage) the situation I am in.

―――――――

Where do I belong today?

Some have left examples for us to follow,
Others lessons for us to learn from,
and the paradox is that many have left both
pain and joy.

—REV. CHRIS ROTHBAUER

Many of us come out of families where addiction or some form of dysfunction was present. Perhaps you had a parent who was a workaholic. Perhaps your grandparent was an alcoholic. Perhaps you have a sibling who is addicted to drugs. In each of these cases, to watch our loved ones suffer is painful. And we are never above that pain—we are right in it. Our lives are affected by the addiction and the dysfunction.

There often comes a point where we cannot take it anymore. The pain becomes too great. The family dynamics are too frustrating. And so we talk to someone about what is going on. We break the silence. It can be awkward at first, our truths coming out in a sputtering of words. Or maybe it is fluid—a long string of sentences pouring out of us so quickly because we have held it all in for so long.

To share our pain, to share the mixed feelings we have, to share the hope or the joy when someone finally gets sober—these are beautiful beginnings in the healing process. These are times when we are showing up for ourselves and really inviting someone in. To share our burdens and our joys with someone else is sacred.

What am I holding on to that can be shared
with another person?

13

Vulnerability gives us freedom, power and connects us to a network of injured souls. It is through the art of being real that we can heal ourself and others.

—SHANNON ALDER

I remember the first time I attended an AA meeting. I was sure I had nothing in common with "those people." I looked around the room and saw people from all walks of life— but none of them, I imagined, were anything like me. Then someone told a story about themselves that hit close to home. It was, in part, my story. She talked about feeling isolated and how she used alcohol to connect with others. She talked about drinking in secret, hiding it from her husband and other family members. She talked about how, in recovery, she learned to be honest with herself and with others. It was as if someone turned on a lightbulb in the dark corners of my spirit.

Alcoholism gives the illusion of separateness. One of its great essential lies is that we are so unique, so special, and our pain is so personal that we simply must drink in order to counter that pain. In recovery, however, we realize that we are, as Alder says, "a network of injured souls." By acknowledging our human struggle, we become more real with ourselves and with others. Our vulnerability to these truths helps us to see ourselves and others more clearly, and as a result, our recovery can begin and continue.

How can I be more real with myself and with others today?

It is not by chance that you arrived here today.
You have been looking for something larger than
yourself.

—Rev. Kimberlee Anne Tomczak Carlson

I have been a Unitarian Universalist since I was a very young child. I think, even then, I was yearning for a place bigger than my own family, something that looked like God working in community, where I could be.

While I didn't have a concept of a "higher power" until much, much later, I still wrestled with the idea of one. I knew I did not like the anthropomorphic version of God.

Once I became active in Twelve-Step work, I was forced to find a Higher Power that worked for me, not just react against others' versions of God. As a result, my connection and dedication to my UU faith has grown stronger and more meaningful.

Where do my Twelve-Step work and my religious
or spiritual commitments intersect?

15

Sometimes what seems most solid and stable is only an illusion of stability. Things that appear more ethereal, that seem to be the toughest to grasp, are in fact the most stable and secure.

—REV. JACKIE CLEMENT

In this process of recovery, many of us learn that we have been operating out of ego, an image that we want others to see, when in truth we have no control over how others see us. This contradiction is an honest truth about ourselves. We would not be struggling with addiction if we did not have some sort of ego issue.

In being vulnerable with someone else, we often learn that though we may think we can easily hold on to our ego, it is not the most stable thing to be operating from. We want people to see us a certain way, and often will do anything to make them do so. But when we let go of the ego, it is freeing. To learn that we are average human beings who make mistakes, who have to live life on life's terms—this is the work of recovery.

And our ego's hold is strong, so we often need the presence of another who has been through the process before. We need their perspective, their guidance, and their experience, strength, and hope to get to a place where we no longer act on false principles and instead grasp something more ethereal—our true selves.

***

How do I want others to see me?

My holy of holies is the human body, health, intelligence, talent, inspiration, love and the most absolute freedom—freedom from violence and lies, no matter what form the latter two take.

—ANTON CHEKHOV

What is your holy of holies? For the alcoholic or addict, it's found in the drugs or alcohol itself. It's the couple seconds of complete and utter freedom that accompanies the first seconds of the high. Then the holy of holies turns into holy hell. If we keep insisting on our addictions long enough, we lose everything. We drink or drug because we want to be free from the confines of our own minds or life's pain, only to discover we have become trapped and enslaved by the very thing we thought would make us free.

The "big book" of Alcoholics Anonymous says that in sobriety "we will know a new freedom and a new happiness." The real holy of holies happens in sobriety when relationships with self and others are healthy and whole; when we are able to think clearly, to follow through on our inspirations, to be more concerned about others than obsessed with ourselves. In order to do this, however, we must let down our guard. We relax and let go. We allow ourselves to become vulnerable to a new way of living. We look for the holy of holies in simple, drama-free daily living.

Where will I find my holy of holies today?

17

Lord, make me an instrument of your peace
Where there is hatred, let me sow love
Where there is injury, pardon
Where there is doubt, faith
Where there is despair, hope
Where there is darkness, light
And where there is sadness, joy

—ATTRIBUTED TO SAINT FRANCIS OF ASSISI

I used to be unwilling to bow my head. I believed it was important for me to show my difference, to not be mistaken for a traditional Christian.

I now think that there was much more to it than that. My ego was such that I couldn't be vulnerable to prayer, that I couldn't humble myself to something I didn't fully understand, that I needed to put on a false front even to myself.

I love Saint Francis's prayer. It takes me outside myself, moves me into gratitude and serenity, takes me to a place of spiritual depth. I love that I have it memorized so that it can accompany me in the middle of the day when I am struggling, or the end of the day so that I can sleep.

Can I allow today's prayer to make me
truly vulnerable?

It has always seemed strange to me. . . . The things we admire in [people], kindness and generosity, openness, honesty, understanding and feeling, are the concomitants of failure in our system. And those traits we detest, sharpness, greed, acquisitiveness, meanness, egotism and self-interest, are the traits of success. And while [people] admire the quality of the first they love the produce of the second.

—JOHN STEINBECK

One of the great aims of recovery is serenity. Many people come into recovery with only the aim to lessen the pain or problems they are experiencing, but, liking the early results, they find that continued recovery and hard work bring an equanimity that begins to produce admirable traits.

I have found a different kind of success by following the principles of recovery. These days, the spiritual principles of honesty and generosity lead me to a quality of serenity that is not so focused on production. I care less about what other people are doing. When I get caught up in feelings of jealousy of what another person has that I do not, I need to go back to find what is happening in me that led to that feeling.

How might I find a new definition of success?

19

Listen, listen, listen to my heart's song. Listen, listen, listen to my heart's song. I will never forsake you, I will never forget you. I will never forsake you, I will never forget you.

—PARAMAHANSA YOGANANDA

This deep feeling of being listened to is such a gift. Throughout my life I have known what it feels like to be listened to and to not really be listened to. We can tell when someone else is listening by their body language, eye contact, engagement, and presence.

As I shared some of my life's story with a trusted fellow, their presence while listening to me was a healing presence. Initially, I felt scared to share these deep secrets about myself. Some of them I had never spoken to another, or had only shared with my most trusted friend. At the end of this Fifth Step process of sharing from the heart and truly being listened to, I felt so much better. It was as if a burden had been lifted. And though there was more work to be done to move toward recovery, the anxiety I had begun with had melted away.

Our listening to one another is a deep gift. It can be the difference between someone continuing to suffer and someone having a healing experience. Your listening is a gift.

Are there people in my life I can offer a listening presence to today?

[Another] way of resisting vulnerability is to practice numbing. Numbing can be anything we use to replace our authentic connections with other human beings.

—REV. THOM BELOTE

When we are alcoholics or addicts, almost anything can make us want to numb ourselves out of feeling our feelings. We drink when we're happy, because unmitigated joy can be overwhelming. We drink when we're sad or depressed, lonely or angry, because those feelings are so powerful we don't know how to handle them without something to "take the edge off."

When we numb ourselves with alcohol or drugs, we fail to honor what life has presented to us. Life happens to all of us. In recovery communities we discover that it is not our great successes that bind us together as humans, but our struggles. We are intimately interconnected with one another—my joy today will one day be yours; your sorrow and grief will one day be mine. As a result, in sobriety we learn, as they say in AA, "to live life on life's terms."

We can only do that, however, by refusing to numb ourselves to these great feelings. Instead, we embrace them, as if they were old friends who have come to visit us. We discover that we don't need to numb ourselves any longer. When we do this, we become fully alive.

———

How will I face and embrace all my feelings today?

21

My high school years were speckled with trust walks. . . . When it was my turn to be blindfolded, I found, while stumbling over gravel in the church parking lot and trudging up the hills behind my church, that despite all efforts to fool me, the whole time I knew exactly where I was.

—RIANNA JOHNSON-LEVY

When I finally made the decision to surrender my life to a power greater than myself, I expected to be on new ground the following day. I expected that life would change overnight, that this act of surrendering would bring me to wholly new territory. Instead, this surrendering brought me a sense of the familiar; it brought me to a place where I felt known.

There had been moments in my life along the way where I had known that feeling of being held by a larger love that never lets us go. In my Unitarian Universalist youth community, in the small church community where I had grown up, in moments of singing together, and in moments of ritual where I was able to close my eyes and trust.

Step Five, to share my personal inventory with a greater power, with myself, and with another human being, was a deep act of trust. It was leaning into the relationship I had with my sponsor, trusting that they would not judge me. As I surrendered to this process, I felt known and understood on a whole new level. I learned how to trust anew.

———————

What are the moments in my life when I have felt safe and protected?

The truth is, everyone is going to hurt you.
You just got to find the ones worth suffering for.
                                        —BOB MARLEY

I used to be good at getting upset and not saying anything. I'd move on with a secret resentment tucked away in my heart (and stomach). Sometimes my behavior was bad, but there was no way I was going to apologize to anyone, for fear my flaws would show. I was also focused on how much other people had hurt me, not on what I had done to others.

Recovery has led me to better behavior. Yes, I can still get hurt, but I am more likely to pause, to consider my part in the situation, to talk to a sponsor about amends I need to make, and to make them.

I also make better choices about new relationships, so that my interactions with others are less volatile. I am glad to go slowly, rather than feeling like I need to have everything right away. As a result, I suffer less.

Where might I demonstrate healthy vulnerability?

23

Wise friend,
words pall and pale before the bounty of your grace
    to me.
God grant that I may be of some small solace
    to you who leave me always so richly dowered
    with joy!

—Rev. Shuma Chakravarty

We struggle with being vulnerable with others. If we didn't, we would probably not be turning to this book. We probably wouldn't be human. Learning to be vulnerable is a lifetime process, one that takes plenty of practice.

We have been holding on to so much. Whether our lives have been touched by addiction, whether we are living with addiction, or whether we suspect addiction is present for us or a loved one, we have been holding so much inside our hearts and minds. What began as an inkling of a thought has gotten bigger and heavier with time. Our wondering became constant thoughts.

And here is the invitation: be brave, reach out, let someone know what you are going through. As we practice sharing of ourselves in meetings and in one-to-one relationships, and in our congregation or spiritual community if we have one, we come to know we can set down worry for longer and longer periods of time. We begin to heal.

What in my life has become a barrier
to being vulnerable with others?

Where do we come from? What are we?
Where are we going?

> —TITLE OF A PAINTING
> BY PAUL GAUGUIN

When I got to the end of Step Five, I felt a real sense of wholeness and completion. I knew in my deepest heart that I had explored every aspect of my life where my addiction had hurt myself and others. No stone was left unturned, nothing left unrevealed.

To be in this place is both freeing and a little scary. Who am I now? Where do I go from here? How do I sit with all of it? If we are fearless and thorough in telling our truths with another, we reveal a good portion of ourselves—pieces of ourselves that we rarely let anyone see. It can feel overwhelming. And it can feel peaceful, both of these at the same time.

To come to this point of completion is to know a vulnerability we may have never known before. This vulnerability brings about a sense of peace in us. And the only thing we are asked to do in this peaceful moment is to sit with it. To sit with all of it. To sit with the things we have just shared, to sit with what we have just done, to get quiet and listen. There is really nothing else to do at the end of this tender, honest, vulnerable time.

What am I called to sit with and
pay attention to today?

25

*Our choice is to inhabit vulnerability as generous
citizens of loss, robustly and fully, or, conversely,
as misers and complainers, reluctant and fearful,
always at the gates of existence but never bravely
and completely attempting to enter, never wanting to
risk ourselves, never walking fully through the door.*

—DAVID WHYTE

That church basement door was one I never wanted to walk through. In fact, I spent nearly the first half of my adult life trying to avoid walking through that door. I was so sure that the moment I walked through that door my life would change forever. I would never know the ease of a casual drink with friends. I would never be happy again. I was 100 percent right on one thing: my life did change the moment I entered an AA meeting and took sobriety seriously. It changed because I was so sick and tired of being sick and tired—of myself, of drinking, of apologies and excuses—that I was ready for a change. My life changed when I began to listen to other people's stories and realized how the disease of alcoholism had affected us all. I began to change as I realized how alcohol had made me miserly of spirit, reluctant and fearful. I began to change as I took new risks with my new companions. I risked asking a person I met if she would be my sponsor that very day. She said yes, and that relationship changed my life. I took one brave step after another, into meetings and coffees and sponsorship and working a program of recovery.

What door do I want to go through today?

That visibility which makes us most vulnerable is that which also is the source of our greatest strength.

—AUDRE LORDE

It is often said in meetings, "Alcohol [or another substance or behavior of choice] is just a symptom of your problems." It's often a cover-up for a kind of pain or unwillingness to uncover our true selves.

I didn't think about vulnerability when I was still in the middle of my addiction. I didn't think about much except for what I felt the world owed me and how I wasn't getting it. I never realized how selfish and self-centered I was, because I was too busy thinking of what I wanted. And I wasn't setting goals; I was changing my desires regularly and not planning for what I wanted.

There is a visibility that comes when living authentically, but it can't come without my taking steps to get there. I can be finally seen for who I am and understood by others. The pain and the true self I had previously tried to cover up are now out in the open for me to claim as my own. I am committed to living each day fully, so that I can get to the source of my strength.

———————

What Step might I examine today in order to allow myself to be authentically visible?

27

We have to live with pain as well as pleasure,
temptation as well as promise,
loneliness as well as love,
fear as well as hope.

—REV. JOHN CORRADO

We must learn to see ourselves as complicated beings rather than one thing or the other. To see ourselves in both a positive and a negative light. To see our amazing brilliance alongside our deepest held sources of shame. We are complicated beings.

Our lives can swing between extremes, out of balance, seeking too much pleasure and also seeking pain that we may think we deserve. In addiction, life can be brought to extremes. Either we are in complete numbness or we are facing the harsh realities of sobriety. We are consumed by the desire for more or we are swearing off it for good. We are good or bad, and finding the in-between can be ever so difficult.

But the truth is that our lives are complicated and they exist in a balance. Some days may be better than others. For the most part, we are a mix of the positive and the negative aspects as well as the neutral and the in-between.

Don't let the voice of either-or or the voice of extremes get the last word. We are multitudes.

———————

Where have I been viewing myself or a life
circumstance in extremes? How can I see myself
or the circumstance as more complex?

Choosing to be curious is choosing to be vulnerable because it requires us to surrender to uncertainty.

—BRENÉ BROWN

When we are in the throes of addiction, we lose the ability to foster a holy curiosity about ourselves. Everything becomes narrowed down to either good or bad, either beautiful or repulsive. In sobriety, our natural curiosity about ourselves and our disease and how it impacts others is awakened. Many a person has found their new vocation in recovery; just as they were supported by others who had been down the path, they now in turn want to help others.

To be curious is to be vulnerable, and to be vulnerable is to surrender to that which we do not know. Surrendering to uncertainty is the only path toward serenity. You know this because you've done it and you've witnessed others doing it as well. As you get farther along the path to sobriety, your curiosity increases. Your sense of wonder expands. And although you don't know the answer to the question "What will happen next?" you greet that question as you do the morning sun: not with shielded eyes or a heavy head, but with a welcoming heart and open arms. This is the path of surrender and serenity. May you take it now.

How can I maintain a holy curiosity today?

29

But I say to you that listen, Love your enemies,
do good to those who hate you, bless those who
curse you, pray for those who abuse you. . . .
Do to others as you would have them do to you.

—LUKE 6:27–29, 31

Anyone who interacts with other people regularly will find themselves tangled in disagreements sometimes. There are going to be people we get along with better than others. Hate is a pretty strong word that I don't use, but it's easy to bring negativity to someone who simply is not my greatest fan.

The Fourth Source of my Unitarian Universalist faith is "Jewish and Christian teachings which call us to respond to God's love by loving our neighbors as ourselves."

I tend to believe, because I am an optimistic UU, that this response comes easily—but when I stop to think of my day-to-day behavior, I realize I am not as good as I think I am. I tend to gossip, or at least vent by sharing my frustrations with others rather than problem solving directly with the other person involved. I am inclined to think the worst rather than assume the best intentions or outcome.

I want to make the words of Luke a morning prayer, and when I fall short, I can make amends, promising to do better.

———

Who needs my blessings and prayers today?

Let us reach the place of self, the place that is not alien to truth. Let us wash over with peace and serenity, with fierce longing for light and heart; with living strength flowing in our veins, bringing ourselves into fearlessness and into trust.

—Rev. Ma Theresa Gustilo Gallardo

Part of Step Five is sharing with ourselves the truth of our actions. This is a part of fearlessly seeking the truth of our experience while also building trust with ourselves. Through our lifetimes, there have been moments when we have needed to live in the lie to keep on going. To build trust with ourselves, we start with listening to our own hearts.

We have places inside of us—secret, sometimes hidden—where we know the truth of who we are and what has happened to us. Giving those places attention is a healing act. Our hearts and spirits become more whole, more integrated. We are no longer fighting the truth of our experiences with questions like "Did I really do that?" or "Was it all that bad?" or even "Did I cause that horrible thing to happen to me?" We honor our truth.

And when we honor our truth, we feel more peaceful, more calm, more at ease. We can live in less fear than we did yesterday, or the day before that, or the day before that. We are at home inside of ourselves.

What small glimpse of truth can I affirm within myself today?

31

People don't like it when you change. Even if that change is making your life better, they don't like it because a little piece of them dies.

—RICKY GERVAIS

"I liked you better when you drank a little," a friend once said to me after I was about six months into sobriety. I was taken aback by that comment. This friend knew how hard I had struggled to come to grips with the fact that I was an alcoholic. I realized that his statement was more about him than it was about me. He liked the person I was when we drank together, because he liked the person *he* was when we drank together. When I got sober, a piece of our friendship died.

When a person gets sober, sometimes friendships can't survive the change. A friendship built around drinking or drugging is usually only skin-deep. However, the next time we got together for a cup of coffee, I told him about my reaction to his comment. He laughed. He said, "You misunderstood me. I said when you drank 'a little,' but my dear, recently you've been drinking a *lot*." What I learned was something the program taught me: absolute, rigorous honesty combined with a willingness to be vulnerable about my feelings. Our friendship continued without alcohol as a common interest.

Who are the friends I surround myself with?
Can I be rigorously honest with them?

June

STEP SIX: WILLINGNESS

Were entirely ready to have
God remove all these defects
of character.

1

I am no bird; and no net ensnares me: I am a free human being with an independent will.

—CHARLOTTE BRONTË

When I was still dating my husband, I once defensively and reactively slammed the car door. We were leaving for a trip and I thought he was telling me that we wouldn't be stopping along the way at rest stops. He pointed out the immaturity of my act.

As a white, cisgender woman, taught by my culture both that I'm generally in the right and that I must defer to men, I wasn't comfortable with the phrase "defects of character" that is commonly used in the Sixth Step of Twelve-Step programs. I think one of the problems I'd been struggling with all my life was defensiveness. I was incredibly frustrated because I felt that I lacked power.

When I could think of the work I needed to do as becoming aware not of my defects, but of where in my life I needed more spiritual maturity, I could then engage in self-improvement. I am grateful to now be able to take more responsible and more adult actions and to be able to use my words to ask for clarification or to assert my needs.

---

*Were there places in my day yesterday where
I could improve on my behavior?*

Your gifts, whatever you discover them to be, can be used to bless or curse the world.

—Rev. Rebecca Ann Parker

When making my list of the defects of character that had been a part of my life, I had to recognize the gifts and the difficulties they had brought me. In being controlling, I had been able to survive, and I had hurt others. In being selfish, I had protected myself in the best way I knew how while also losing touch with how to care for others. In being dishonest, I had been able to navigate an abusive environment, and I had lied to those I love and care about the most. Before letting all of this go, I had to embrace the ways these defects had hurt me and the ways they had served me.

When I first heard about this part of recovery where I would name my character defects, it sounded like a bad idea. Growing up in an alcoholic home, I already had internalized a lot of shame. Didn't I feel bad enough already? Doesn't my Unitarian Universalist faith call me to value the inherent worth and dignity of every person—including myself? But this process is not meant to reinforce the bad feelings we have about ourselves. Instead, it invites us to look at the ways our defects have been used to both bless and curse the world. It can help us recognize our assets and gifts, to embrace the good things about ourselves alongside those we are not proud of.

What is one part of me that I can see as both a blessing and a curse?

3

I have learned over the years that when one's mind is made up, this diminishes fear.

—ROSA PARKS

It was a sunny day in my city. I woke up feeling light of heart and spirit. It was a morning in early autumn. And I looked around me and felt connected to the world, to all existence, in a way I'd never felt before. Everything was in a state of equilibrium, with a gentle calm about it, and there I was, a part of that balance, that serenity.

I remember that moment. It was some months into my sobriety, when fear, anxiety, neediness, pain, and shame had been bubbling up in my consciousness, and in that moment, they vanished! I had only begun to work the Steps of my recovery. I hit just about ninety meetings in ninety days, as I was told to do—yes, I listened to someone else's wisdom, my sponsor's.

That sunny-day experience sticks with me these many years later. It is the spirit with which I came to approach letting my Higher Power remove my defects of character.

I found I had to move into Step Six the same way I clean my closet: by taking everything out of the closet of my mind and heart. In essence, I had to make three piles: the characteristics that were positive and worth keeping, the characteristics that caused me and others problems, and those I wasn't sure about. It's not as quick a process as cleaning out my clothes closet, but it was a pretty good process.

How do I want to approach and enter Step Six?

I, myself, am made entirely of flaws, stitched together with good intentions.

—AUGUSTEN BURROUGHS

Step Six is similar to Step One in that both require an awareness. While the First Step required us to recognize that we were powerless over our addiction, the Sixth Step invites us to say, "Okay, I'd like something different here. The way I think and act doesn't serve me or the world as well as it could."

It's spiritual work, in that I don't believe that it's possible to say this one time and have everything be suddenly okay. The philosopher William James pointed out, "The greatest discovery of any generation is that a human can alter [their] life by altering [their] attitude." So each day, when I arise, I am wise when I make a conscious effort to be aware of what I think, say, and do.

What prayer or meditation could point me to a positive attitude?

5

When you do things from your soul,
you feel a river moving in you, a joy.
—RUMI

My willingness to have my defects removed by my Higher Power was always either a flippant request or a move of desperation. Even into the earlier years of recovery I wasn't entirely conscious of the need to release myself from an impossible task: to remove my defects by myself, through self-will. And it's an imperfect path, with nettles and pitfalls along the way, but there are more times and more moments of a conscious awareness that I cannot do better or be better on my own.

My communities of healing and my Higher Power give me strength when I am weak, insight when I am obtuse, and a helping hand when I have fallen back into "me" instead of "we." Becoming willing isn't a one-shot deal. It happens in moments, again and again, with aid from others and a big dose of humility. It is worthy work, and hope is not idle.

———————

What shall I do today to bring my focus to my
deeper self? From that place in me, how shall I open
my heart and soul to the boundless healing power
of the Creative Force known by many names?
Am I willing to be healing to my core and joyful?

I refused the hand of one who reached out to me,
clinging instead to old familiar ways. I chose to
remain stuck inside a problem, rather than ask for
help to solve it.

—REV. ELIZABETH TARBOX

When I first entered into a recovery room, I was not really excited about admitting I was an addict. Each person who shared began with the line "Hi, my name is _____ and I'm a compulsive overeater." Or "I'm an alcoholic." Or even "I'm an adult child of an alcoholic." As I listened to folks sharing, I found so many reasons for ways I was not like them: I was not that bad off. I had not gone as far in my addiction as they had.

But here I was. Willing enough to get to the meeting but not willing to identify with addiction . . . yet.

The willingness came when I was able to listen to the stories and experiences being shared and to identify with them. Slowly but surely, someone told my story, and then someone else told a story eerily similar to my own. The connections were made over time. And I was able to reach out for help, even when I had begun as someone completely unwilling to have it.

What am I unwilling to face about myself?

7

Be willing to be a beginner every single morning.
—MEISTER ECKHART

I've had days where things went wrong from the minute I got up. The coffee grounds spilled all over the floor, or the coffee filter was folded over and water filled the counter and flowed down the cabinets.

There's a tool used in many Twelve-Step materials that says, "On awakening let us think about the twenty-four hours ahead. We consider our plans for the day." Each day is an opportunity to start again.

Before I entered recovery, messed up coffee would have ruined my entire day. I would have screamed and yelled, blamed the coffee maker and probably someone else in my house, and I would have used this one small accident to become a very big thing. I would also have been frustrated because I liked to think I didn't make mistakes. I was a coffee-making expert. Now, I carry a beginner's mind and I am gifted with serenity.

I can decide to start my day over any time. Even as early as 7 a.m.

---

*How can I be willing to be a beginner
this morning?*

Were entirely ready to have God remove all these defects of character.

—SIXTH STEP

My Universalist theological heritage states again and again that all are loved by a loving Higher Power. Step Six does not mean that defects of character place us beyond the love of God or even the love of humanity. Instead, becoming entirely ready means accepting that our Higher Power loved us with these shortcomings. Our Higher Power loved us through the experience of discovering these character defects through honesty. And we are becoming ready to let go these parts of ourselves that we developed as a way to survive but that eventually led to our being disconnected from those around us and from God.

The Sixth Step asks us whether we are entirely ready to say goodbye to the parts of us keeping us blocked and disconnected. Becoming ready is checking in about whether or not you trust that which is greater than yourself to change you, to love you through it all. In that trust, in believing that that love is real and it is for all of us, we become entirely ready.

What am I holding on to that blocks me from connecting with others?

Pain is never unending, as long as you remember its limitations and do not indulge in fanciful exaggeration.

—EPICTETUS

When I drank, I hid my fear of others. I'd been taught that our family was different, and not in a good way. Family secrets were to be kept—though no one ever said so out loud. If other people knew, they'd think the worst of me. It was only in sobriety and with the help of therapy that I found my way through a lot of that. Making friends has never been easy for me, and while I can't say it is easy now, it's better.

Part of my work in Step Six was to be clear about what was me and my character defects and what was false information I was fed as a child or interpreted incorrectly growing up. I needed to repeat my personal inventory steps, in a kind of review, in the movement toward becoming willing to let go of what was mine to let go of.

What is the cause of my residual pain? Is it real or a ghost of the past? Is it related to my character defects? How do I still use past pain to excuse poor choices?

*In truth, feminism is flawed because it is a movement
powered by people and people are inherently flawed.*

—Roxane Gay

Today I am waking up with an appreciation for the ability
to acknowledge all that is in the world. I'm not going to give
up on things that are flawed because the world is flawed.
When I become aware of this fact, I feel more alive.

I feel ready to address my shortcomings, many of which
show up in clear patterns. I used to think I didn't lie, because
I didn't steal money or cheat on my taxes. But as I've continued to practice, I've found that I use a more sly deceitfulness
and manipulation to meet my selfish needs.

---

*Am I entirely ready to give up something
I've been ignoring?*

11

I am open and I am willing,
For to be hopeless would seem so strange.
It dishonors those who came before us,
So lift me up to the light of change.

—HOLLY NEAR

Who am I to say that recovery is not possible for me? So many others have traveled this road before, and they are there, at the ready, to share the ways they have struggled and the ways they have been led to persist. There is so much hope in these experiences, so many valuable learnings from those who have gone before.

To think that I am beyond help is to think that I am above or below others. Either I am better than them, because I am not in their life circumstances or am beyond what they needed to get sober, or I am less than them, a hopeless case, unworthy of anyone's caring or attention. If I am honest, I usually find myself in some mixture of these two mindsets. Either way, I remain in my addiction and unable to accept any help.

We honor those who came before us when we are open and honest enough to say, "Yes. I too am one of you. And I am willing to accept the help you have to offer." Let this moment be a beginning for us.

Can I list those I know who care about me or who
have healed from addiction? Can I keep this list
with me in my pocket as a reminder of those
who have gone before?

I avoid looking forward or backward, and try to keep looking upward.

—CHARLOTTE BRONTË

I approached Step Six the first time wanting to believe that, somehow, all the things I'd done that I felt pain and shame about would be lifted off of me, bringing me to another level beyond my Fourth and Fifth Step journeys. It would be a cleansing of the corners that I might have overlooked before. Instead, it was another level, all right, but of my own awakening. History would not change, would not be erased, but going forward I could hope to live conscious of my brokenness, with better tools and a clear focus on my Higher Power's love, and do better.

What do I need to do today to help me accept what was—neither overdramatizing nor minimizing it— and prepare for what my Higher Power's love promises?

13

Our willingness to acknowledge that we only see half the picture creates the conditions that make us more attractive to others. The more sincerely we acknowledge our need for their different insights and perspectives, the more they will be magnetized to join us.

—MARGARET WHEATLEY

Willingness in the literature of AA comes up a lot in the Third Step, in which we make a decision to change our lives by changing our attitude. But willingness is always present, including in Step Six, when we become willing to have God (or however you name that thing that is greater than you) remove our defects of character. There's a maxim, used in recovery and in Buddhism, that says, "Drop the rock." It means that we'll never be able to let go of our flawed behavior as long as we hold it tight.

Willingness is essential for me to make any change in my life. Nothing is going to happen if I'm not willing. I can't get to the gym, can't write that sermon, can't clean up my office if I'm not willing. How brilliant is it to have a Step simply focused on willingness?

What am I willing to do today that I wasn't yesterday?

My work often stems from one question: What do I need to hear? . . . It is the happy coincidence of being human that other people can also find comfort and courage and steadiness in the things I write.

—JESS REYNOLDS

A big part of taking the Sixth Step is accepting our own humanity. Each one of us is fallible, fragile, full of failures and successes, ordinary and miraculous all at the same time. To become willing to have a power greater than ourselves remove our shortcomings, we must first accept them as a truth of our humanity. There have been times when we have disappointed, hurt, and even harmed others and acted solely in our own interest.

No human can get through life without falling short. Unitarian Universalists often talk about how good and amazing human beings are. We also need to make room for the difficult aspects of being human, for the parts of ourselves we would rather not show others.

So here we are. Laid bare, in a way. Our shortcomings listed before us. Our past actions are sealed in our memories. What choice do we have but to take an honest look at the entire picture of who we are? In honoring our whole selves, we experience freedom, healing, and humility in ways we could have never expected.

Where have I fallen short this week?

15

Faith is taking the first step even when you don't see the whole staircase.
— Rev. Martin Luther King Jr.

Do I have to believe in God to give myself over to Step Six?

Today I have faith in something I was not willing to have faith in as I practiced my addiction. I have come to believe in something beyond my own ego and self-will. As I have come to believe in my authentic self, I have come to understand that something beyond my ego, will, and smarts has brought me this far.

Whether you see God as the Ultimate Source or as a metaphor for the creative force, or if you don't use the term at all, I can't afford to argue about it. It's more important to my recovery that I do the footwork that I believe any force for good would have me do; I don't think God, or whoever, is interested in credit!

What I need are the tools that help me to heal in order to live a healthy and principled life, however imperfectly. There are different ways of knowing something. Knowing there's a power greater than myself isn't the same thing as knowing a chair is a chair or a bottle is a bottle, but it's at least as important. I rely upon that kind of knowledge to work the Steps of my recovery.

Do I believe in a power greater than myself?
How do I rely upon that belief in my recovery
each day?

When you heard that voice and
knew finally it called for you
and what it was saying—where
were you?

—REV. NANCY SHAFFER

Can you sit down for a minute in peace and answer the question of how you were called? What you were called to?

Are you willing today to reply to something that is not yet clear but is inviting you on this journey?

On this beautiful day, I am willing to begin, to know that it takes whatever it takes. Right in the middle of the year, in the middle of the calendar, in the middle of things, I need to find the willingness to listen to something both deeply inside and outside myself, so that I can begin to see what parts of me are keeping me from discovering who I am truly meant to be.

I think that being "called" means hearing something that I might have shoved down deeply. It needs to come out.

———————

What does the voice say to me today?

17

We are not alone. Any act one of us will choose must change other lives. Just as every act others choose changes our own lives.

—REV. JOEL MILLER

I come from a long line of folks who have lived and died in addiction. Generations of people who have mostly been alcoholics but probably also were addicted to food, gambling, sex, excitement, work, and a few other things. It makes sense that I too lived with addiction and the effects of addiction. This had been a part of our family makeup for decades, each generation passing it on to the next and on to the next.

When I made the choice to get into recovery, a cycle was broken. Not to say I have fixed my family or that I am now better than those who came before. No. It is my hope that my finding healing in my own heart and spirit may make the burden on the next generation a little easier. And then the generation after that one might suffer in addiction and addictive behaviors a little less. Perhaps, through my getting into recovery, a future generation may experience more ease around this disease.

My life and my relationships with the folks I care about have been transformed. I work better with others, I am a better spouse and friend now that I am in recovery. That in and of itself makes all the difference in the world.

What is one choice I can make today to support my own health and well-being?

Soul is about authenticity. Soul is about finding the things in your life that are real and pure.

—JOHN LEGEND

There's a point at which I started to believe in myself. I wanted to be more authentic and let go of both the good and the bad of what others thought of me, because I realized that what I thought of myself—my own attitudes and behaviors—was what mattered.

When other people attributed what I've come to understand as my diseased behavior to my creative spirit, I took refuge in that. It gave me permission to behave that way. And when still others found the greatest fault in my behavior, I was all too ready to take their judgments to heart. I didn't dare look honestly at myself.

Maybe it's impossible to be 100 percent willing to have all my defects removed. I kind of liked some of them—especially when I didn't look closely at how some of my attitudes and behaviors were hurtful to others or myself.

This work is about having faith that I *can* let my defects go and that my Higher Power *can* remove them. And, yes, I can take them back in any moment, being human. It is then that I must choose how to proceed. I want to be truly myself, authentic, and whole, and it's part of my daily spiritual work.

———

Am I willing to believe that I can be more authentically myself and, with the help of my Higher Power, let go of my defects of character?

19

Sabbath implies a willingness to be surprised by unexpected grace, to partake of those potent moments when creation renews itself, when what is finished inevitably recedes, and the sacred forces of healing astonish us with the unending promise of love and life.

—WAYNE MULLER

Neither the idea nor the observation of Sabbath is popular these days, as either a religious or a spiritual practice. But those who do practice are imbued with gifts that can't be found when never taking a break other than a short sleep.

Parents of young children often set aside time to be free of phones, tablets, and similar devices. Not only does this help with sleeping and eating habits, it also helps the family develop closer and deeper bonds. Screen-free time can do the same for adults.

My Sabbath time has allowed me freedom from 24/7 work, from a forced sense of productivity, and from social media and email that provide a never-ending string of things to respond to. It can be a time to read, be in nature, spend time with friends and loved ones. It has become a force for healing.

Am I willing to engage in a Sabbath away from work and screens?

Do not curse me to perish with all my dreams fulfilled.
Do not afflict me with a vision so narrow and a heart
so small,
That all my greatest hopes could be accomplished
within a single lifetime.

—Rev. Kelly Weisman Asprooth-Jackson

This life and its possibilities are so much more expansive than what we can see from our limited perspective. It may feel in this moment like there is only one road for us, only one path we can go down. It may feel like we do not have a choice or that we are victims of circumstances beyond our control. And some of that may be true. And yet more is possible than we can ever imagine.

When we are willing to put down an addictive substance, we are saying more is possible for us. We are saying that our life doesn't need to be dictated by that substance, that our life is worth more than chasing an effect.

When we put down those substances, we have the chance to pick up hope, to pick up possibility, to pick up a different set of tools than the ones we have been working with thus far. Our lives can be lived along spiritual lines—lines of connection and sustenance. We don't have to be cut off from possibility and hope anymore.

What am I willing to believe is possible
for me today?

21

*Willingness, honesty, and open mindedness
are the essentials of recovery.*

—ALCOHOLICS ANONYMOUS,
"THE BIG BOOK"

As abstract virtues, willingness, honesty, and open-mindedness were certainly life values I could sign on to. But when it came to my addiction? Well, that was a bit tricky.

For so long, my addiction thrived in secrecy and dishonesty with myself. It was hard to admit that I had been causing myself harm all those years, when to use had felt so good and had made life bearable. It was difficult at first to even be willing to admit that I had an addiction, let alone ask for help to address it. When it came to my addiction, I did not believe anyone or anything could really help me to get sober. Sobriety felt impossible.

When I was ready to be honest, when I was willing to change, when my mind was open about what kind of healing was possible, amazing things began to happen. I grew spiritually in ways I had never imagined before. I was able to tell the truth of my experience, no longer holding my addiction in secrecy or shame. I was freed from the life I had lived before and entered into a new phase of my existence.

---

*Where am I being called to be honest about
my experience today in order to be healed
from secrecy and shame?*

The willingness to open to depth is the chief way in which dignity and purpose return to life.

—JAMES HOLLIS

First I must be willing and then willing to be open. I have found that the depth comes on its own, after I make myself available to finding a better way to live.

I have found that people don't usually get engaged in any kind of recovery until their life becomes unmanageable (or too painful) the way it is. There is often a crack that gets opened and a feeling, "I don't want to live this way anymore," that allows something different to come in.

At first, there is just the noticing that I'm not doing this alone. Then that others seem happy. Then later, often upon reflection, that I have found dignity and hope and meaning in my life.

Willingness is the key.

———

Today, what part of my life am I open to seeing?

23

But if you wait until you feel fully ready
you may never take the leap at all
and Infinity is calling you forth
out of this birth canal
and into the future's wide expanse.

—RABBI RACHEL BARENBLAT

There's always an excuse not to grace the doors of the space that is there to help you. Perhaps you don't quite yet have your stuff together in the way you would like. Perhaps your appearance is a little messier than you'd like to show to others. Perhaps you have done things that are unforgivable and that, if you can just figure out how to undo them, then you'll be ready to receive the help. Perhaps the addiction or the behavior hasn't gotten so bad that you can't stand living with yourself anymore. But once you get there, you'll go through those doors.

Perfectionism is such a thief. It robs us of experiences we could be having, of growth we could be experiencing, of the help we so desperately need right now. If anyone feels perfectly anything as they reach out in the midst of a desperate moment, they are telling you a lie and they are lying to themselves. The moment of asking for help is a tender moment.

You may not be perfect, but the help and support are there for you anyway. So you may as well not wait for the perfect moment and just reach out to let folks know what you need.

Where have I been waiting for the perfect moment?

*See the evidence. Ignore your intuition. Swallow
your emotions. Reason away the evidence.
Pretend all is well.*

—PAUL COLAIANNI,
"DENIAL IN FIVE EASY STEPS"

There is no denying there are many ills in this life. This is reality. It's also true that there is great beauty, wonder, and kindness. In my earliest years of recovery I gave much more power to the negative, especially about myself and my corner of the world. Seeing the glass as half-empty seemed to come most naturally to me.

I was never a happy drunk. Denial was a cloak I hid behind. I was working or in school; wasn't I okay? Like so many of us, I was quite resourceful in coming up with reasons to justify my poor choices. Truths that I'd rather not face, or that were in conflict with the truth I intuitively knew but did not wish to accept, stayed packed away in a far, dark corner. My wrongs were the worst—even if another person would have assured me that that wasn't nearly true!

When we are truly willing to expect a miracle, we can ask for relief. We will then be able to notice when those character defects begin to show themselves again.

———

*Am I willing to accept the positives as well as the
defects of my character? Can I seek the Source that
has helped me so far in recovery and ask for relief?*

25

Yet we had been seeing another kind of flight, a spiritual liberation from this world, people who rose above their problems. They said God made these things possible, and we only smiled. We had seen spiritual release, but liked to tell ourselves it wasn't true.

—ALCOHOLICS ANONYMOUS,
"THE BIG BOOK"

Today I am going to see the glass as half full. I choose to believe that there is some larger energy that is not me, and that the deepest inner me can remove those pesky personal flaws to which the other trivial part of me clings. I can believe that a Higher Power exists outside of me and is larger than I am, but also that I can access it through my own consciousness, "for deep down inside every [person] is the fundamental idea of God."

Sometimes the mystical and the scientific truths are just what I need to help me realize that I am living here, now, to be of use to the world. Even on a day when I face difficulties, I can choose the best part of myself to respond to those difficulties.

I am here in this place that is often much better than the past but that still has a way to go before reaching the Beloved Community. There is much to do, and some of it is mine.

What purpose might I have for this day?

Just because something was a certain way for many years doesn't mean we have to continue. Traditions and habits can be changed or broken and that's not always bad. It doesn't mean we didn't learn or like what we did in the past, it just means that we moved on to something else and that's okay too.

—RAYLA D. MATTSON

I am so grateful for the human capacity to grow and heal. I am grateful that we are able to look upon the past and see where our traditions and habits made us who we are. And I am grateful for the capacity and the willingness to be open to change.

I would not be who I am today if I was not willing to be changed. It isn't a judgment of where I have come from. I wanted things to be different. I desired change because the life I was living was not the one I wanted to be living. I knew I could not experience the life I dreamed of without first being open to some kind of change in habits, thought patterns, emotional responses, and spiritual orientation.

And my life changed, took a different direction, in ways I could never have imagined. When we let go of the old ways, sometimes changes sneak in there that we couldn't foresee or predict. I can tell you that I would not trade my life today for the old ways any day.

When have I left traditions and old habits behind for a new experience?

27

I think our capacity for wholeheartedness can never be greater than our willingness to be broken-hearted. It means engaging with the world from a place of vulnerability and worthiness.

—BRENÉ BROWN

We come to recovery from many different life circumstances. To reach Step Six we had to be willing to work through the first five, whether wholeheartedly or begrudgingly, because our sponsor told us to. to. Those of us who suffered abuse of any kind, whether inflicted by trusted family or strangers, may have a hard time surrendering ourselves to a Higher Power at every turn.

Trust is so fragile, and the veins of profound shame and self-blame run to the core. We tell ourselves "no blame, no shame"; that is, it wasn't our fault we were abused, and we needn't feel shame about it either. As right as that may sound, we may not be ready to believe it. To let God or our Higher Power remove all our defects requires that we be open and vulnerable yet again, and that's a challenge for us. The promise Step Six holds can sound hollow at first reflection. We want to be willing, but sometimes our fear, pain, shame, and self-blame can stand in the way. We mustn't rush to and through Step Six. There are no short-cuts worth taking.

Can I work on my relationship with God, with my Higher Power, to create the space and trust I need to engage with Step Six?

How do we hold people accountable for wrongdoing and yet at the same time remain in touch with their humanity enough to believe in their capacity to be transformed?

—BELL HOOKS

For all the work I'd done to this point, I know I approached Step Six unsure more about myself than about anything having to do with a Higher Power.

My first questions were all about myself: did I deserve to have my defects of character removed? Were my faults too many, too terrible? Weren't the things I'd done, or failed to do, so bad that I didn't deserve goodness? Were my faults like barnacles on a ship, which could be scrubbed off when the ship reached port? Or were they just a part of me, intrinsic to my being? The questions I wasn't letting myself ask—but which were alive and powerful within me—were harsher: Was I willing? How could I be ready, let alone entirely ready, if I didn't believe in my own humanity and that I was worthy?

Little did I understand that I didn't need to understand Step Six at all! All that was needed was to surrender to the process and trust that what I needed to learn or gain or experience would be revealed to me.

Can I release the compulsion to understand why or how a Higher Power can work in my life? Can I surrender and accept my own humanity?

29

If your compassion does not include yourself, it is incomplete.

—JACK KORNFIELD

It's so easy to confuse willingness and willfulness. Willfulness means that a mind is set on something. In its destructive form, the human will can forge ahead concerned only with a goal, without considering how one gets there. Willfulness can be a kind of stubbornness, the kind that helped get many of us in trouble.

Willingness comes from another aspect of us. Call it heart. Call it spirit. Call it soul. It comes from a place deep inside: not the top of the head, but the core of our being. We can begin to let ourselves into that space more often as we work through the Steps. We can let our willingness be calm, cultivated, and considered, not driven or reactive. It is through compassion for ourselves that we can be released from the bonds of ego.

Can I pay attention today to what generates my reactivity and take a different course? Can I allow myself to notice the ways I can show myself compassion, calm my spirit, and consider my actions before I take them?

Fill me with anxiety, O Life!
Electrify me, make me nervous
Beyond any staid concern
For those things which challenge
Placid, flaccid ways, anachronisms of being.

—ARTHUR GRAHAM

There is value in seeing the positives as well as the negatives of our character defects. Fear can be a valuable creative force. Dishonesty could have been a survival skill and may derive from compassion for another. Anger is a healthy expression of human emotion. Our judgments can be a way to check our guts. And all of these are useful to us in some way.

To become willing to let them go, we must acknowledge the gift they have been. And we also have to acknowledge that perhaps we need not to stop experiencing fear, dishonesty, anger, and judgment but rather to change our relationship with them.

Expecting ourselves to have no character defects is inhumane. We need to seek balance in our lives. Not to be ruled by anxiety at all times but to see where it is helpful in keeping us safe and fueling creativity. Not to go quickly from anger to rage in ways that hurt but to be angry as an honest expression of our emotions. May we seek the both/and of our character defects and be willing to be transformed in our relationship to them.

What are some of the positive aspects of things I
think I need to change in myself?

July

STEP SEVEN: HUMILITY

Humbly asked God to remove

our shortcomings.

1

*We cast what we must
change about ourselves
onto the waters flowing
to the sea. The sins,*

*errors, bad habits, whatever
you call them, dissolve.*
      —MARGE PIERCY

Religion has developed many ceremonies, rituals, and holidays to help us let go of the untoward things we have done, the mistakes we have made, the flaws in our character. It's as though we need the calendar date, the excuse, the ritual in order to make the change.

In Twelve-Step work, the Seventh Step suggests humility as a virtue and invites us to a willingness to change. It's often called self-centered fear, that thing that keeps us holding on to the safe and comfortable.

Sometimes we need to hear someone tell us to "drop the rock" before we are able to cast off what we must.

What am I willing to drop into the flowing waters?

I don't want to belong to any club that would
accept me as one of its members.

—GROUCHO MARX

I am a reluctant Al-Anon. Why would anyone want to join this club? I discovered that I didn't want to join, but I choose to join this club again and again each day.

My adult child has been drinking since they were fifteen or sixteen, for more than ten years now. At first, I thought all of my established spiritual practices would help. I meditated. I prayed.

What I also discovered is that I had made a bargain with the God of my understanding. I believed that I had suffered enough in childhood and that my children would be somehow protected by this bargain I had made with God.

I begin each new year by participating in a burning bowl ritual. Some practice the ritual with two pieces of paper, writing on one the old things they want to let go of and on the other the new things they want to create. Both papers are then burned in the bowl. I prefer writing what I'm willing to let go of and burning just that. I'm becoming more comfortable with burning both the past and the future. Willing to let go of the old, I am also willing to let go of what I think the future will look like. There is no guarantee that my life will look the way I want it to, no matter how much hard work or deep healing that I do.

What am I willing to let go of, from both the past
and the future I think I know?

3

*I want to be better than I am in the responsibilities
  that are mine:
I am conscious of many petty resentments.
I am conscious of increasing hostility toward
  certain people.*

—REV. HOWARD THURMAN

In the pursuit of appearing to be a "good person," I had many secrets. I thought things I would never say aloud. I held onto grudges for years. I silently harbored resentments that festered, never succeeding in getting those around me to change. To keep up appearances as a good person is exhausting. And it is soul-sucking. I came into recovery so sick from all of these things I was holding on the inside.

To be humble is to be honest about who we are. Not to put ourselves down, but to be truly honest about our fears and resentments and the ways we have lived out of right relationship.

It was a humbling process to face the many things I did not want others to see about me. And it was a healing process. Keeping all these things inside was so hard—it left my brain abuzz with fear and anxiety constantly, even while I had a smile on my face. Letting them out helped me to live a more integrated, honest, and authentic life. What a blessing.

———————

*What am I keeping inside that I need to share
with another person?*

Humanist teachings which counsel us to heed the guidance of reason and the results of science, and warn us against idolatries of the mind and spirit.

—FIFTH SOURCE OF
UNITARIAN UNIVERSALISM

An important inspiration for Unitarian Universalist faith comes from the fifth of the Six Sources of our living tradition. We are reminded that reason and science both add to ongoing truth, and it is a gift to be able to take notice of them.

The warning against idolatry is helpful to me because it helps me avoid an individual (or group) tendency to jump to conclusions or to be arrogant in faith or behavior.

The great Unitarian ethicist James Luther Adams wrote, "Idolatry occurs when a social movement adopts as the center of loyalty an idol, a segment of reality torn away from the context of universality, an inflated, misplaced abstraction made into an absolute."

I can use this wisdom from Unitarian Universalism as a reminder not to take my view as the only view, not to use the partial for the whole, not to make a person my Higher Power.

Am I making an idol of my beliefs or behavior?

Religion is humility before the universe.

—Anonymous

I find comfort in the three Cs: "I didn't cause it. I can't control it. I can't cure it." At first I spent a lot of time blaming myself. I have so much practice being a victim; it was easy to believe that I had caused my loved one's alcoholism and that this was one more thing that was wrong with me.

My victimhood stood in the way of naming my other shortcomings, so it was the first one that had to go. Humility felt like blame. Humility felt like shame, but it isn't. The word *humility* comes from the root word *humus*, which means earth. If you have ever held the ashes of a loved one, you know why we say "Ashes to ashes, dust to dust" at a graveside. Once, many years ago, holding the remains of someone I loved and spreading them at the graveside of an ancestor, I learned to lean into humility before the universe.

My family member's alcoholism is not more evidence that I am inherently damaged. My family member's alcoholism is a reminder that I am not in charge here. I am always in a sort of free-fall toward surrender. If I stop the free-fall and step out onto the ledge looking for someone to fix, change, or influence, I forget my place in the universe. I forget that humility teaches me to be in awe of all that I did not cause, I cannot control, and I cannot cure.

What does humility teach me?

May the mantle of humility give courage to admit when we are wrong.

—REV. MAUREEN KILLORAN

Step Seven asks us to humbly ask God to remove our defects of character. When I was working this Step, my sponsor gave me a list of character defects and their opposites. She asked me to take a look at all of them and to select a top twenty that seemed to be recurring patterns for me. I circled many. Then she told me to write the defects and their opposites on a card and pray for God to remove each defect that I might live more in its opposite.

And this practice led to many hard lessons. When I was asking that my gossiping behavior be removed, that I might be more close-mouthed, kind, and praising, a friend reached out to me to let me know how my gossiping behavior had hurt them. When I prayed to have my judgmental nature removed, that I might be more humble and considerate, moments when I sat in judgment of others became more painful. It was a transformation I had thought I wanted, but it turned out to be much more difficult than I had originally thought.

But here's the deal: in all of this I am living a much better life than I was before, when I was heedlessly unaware of the ways my actions were harming others. I am learning from moments when I am wrong and growing in ways I could never have imagined.

———

Where am I making room to learn from my shortcomings?

7

Creation is too grand, complex, and mysterious to be captured in a narrow creed. That is why we cherish individual freedom of belief.

—REV. WILLIAM SCHULZ

Unitarian Universalists are specifically called to humility. Our Third Source affirms the wisdom of the world's religions, which inspires us in our spiritual and ethical life. As UUs we avow the wisdom of pluralism and its potential to bring about a better world.

When I remember this in my behavior, I can stay open and willing to learn. I have a great appreciation for the complexities of the world and my place in them. But in my concern to get things done, I sometimes forget the beauty of hearing multiple opinions, of taking time to make decisions, of not always knowing where we're going.

I practice humility by remembering each person's freedom in Unitarian Universalism to find their own truth. Together.

―――――――――

How am I inspired by the world's religions to move toward humility?

We are all more human than otherwise.
—REV. RICHARD S. GILBERT

Being so very human, I cringe each time I hear that alcoholism is a family disease. If I have inherent worth and dignity, as my Unitarian Universalist Principles declare, then how is it that I have to "humbly ask for the removal of my shortcomings"? Can't I affirm my worth and dignity instead? Can't I just blame the alcoholic in my life and move on?

Of course it's hard to move on when we are caught in blame. Unitarian Universalists know that "what affects one, affects us all." Practicing the Twelve Steps reminds me that as I heal, so others will heal. I humbly ask my Higher Power to remove my shortcomings because they keep me stuck.

Alcoholism is a family disease. When I respond to the alcoholic in my life, I bring my whole self. I bring both my worth and my shortcomings. My shortcomings don't make me worthless; they make me human. As I see them more clearly, I see myself more clearly. As I see myself more clearly, I become grateful for this family disease that shapes me and, paradoxically, heals me.

———————

*What gifts have I received from the family
disease of alcoholism?*

9

It's not about who you know. Enlightenment comes from within. The Dalai Lama texted me that.

—TAHANI AL-JAMIL,
IN *THE GOOD PLACE*

New arrivals in Twelve-Step groups are often told that one way to develop a bit of humility is to do something good without letting anyone know you did it. That feels counterintuitive, because you'll want to let people know as soon as you've accomplished that good thing. And how can we know what good things to do if we've never done things like that before?

Should I put away someone's cart in the grocery store? What if someone sees me and thinks I'm great? Should I buy coffee for the person behind me in line? Will the barista be impressed? Should I be like David Sedaris and pick up the trash in my neighborhood—and then write a book about it?

See? It's not as easy as it looks. But neither is humility. It may take some time to do the right thing without thinking of appearances or impressing someone, but the time it takes will be worth it.

———————

*What can I do today without expecting
an external reward?*

Those humble places.
The quiet, still spaces where
I am held in
A love greater than myself.
　　　　—ALEX JENSEN

It is a great spiritual discovery to find oneself right-sized. Not big enough to be ruler over everything or even just other people's lives. Not small enough that we are nothing and have no value or worth. But right-sized. Human-sized. Imperfect. Humble. Sometimes right and sometimes wrong. Having power alongside others rather than power-over or even power-under.

Here we are open to learning and open to the Spirit, which some choose to call God. In remaining open, we can make our way through our days, allowing what may come to come. Allowing our day to unfold without our designs and plans for those around us getting in the way.

May we find these humble places, these right-sized spaces, these human-sized graces for ourselves and for one another.

———————

What is my relationship to humility?

11

*I pray because, alone, I am not enough and also
    I am too much. . . .
When I pray, I acknowledge that God is not me.*

—REV. ROGER COWAN

In her autobiographical television miniseries *Out on a Limb*, actress Shirley MacLaine famously shouted on a beach, "I am God!" We, a generation of seekers and enthusiasts, desperately wanted to be the God of our own lives and others' lives. We desperately wanted to be in control.

I am, however, connected to all of humankind and all creation. We always need a reminder of this oneness. It took a famous person standing on a beach shouting "I am God" to remind us to love ourselves. It took someone shouting "I am God" for us to see the danger of that statement when it is shouted without humility.

When I pray, I acknowledge that there is something beyond me that has the reins. I wish there were a God that would reach in and fix my problems, but I don't think that such a God exists. I would like to worship something that would protect me from further suffering, but I don't think that such a God exists. When I pray, I acknowledge that so much of life remains in mystery. When I pray, I acknowledge that God is not me and I am not responsible for the alcoholic.

What happens when I pray?

Cultivate humility and equanimity. Humility in the face of the mystery helps us with the frustration we often feel when we think we are supposed to know it all and be in control of it all, when really we're not.

—RAM DAS

When Ram Das said this, he was speaking of sitting with a loved one who is dying.

Years ago, before my loved one became an alcoholic, I worked in a recovery program for indigent women and adolescents. Looking back, I have to wonder at a universe that may have been preparing me for what was to come. One year I met a man who encouraged me to adapt the Twelve Steps for women, especially women of color. He mentioned that many in the field had begun to question how the program, which had been originally designed for white men by white men, could work for marginalized populations. After all, those at the margins already feel disempowered.

I rewrote the Twelve Steps as part of a paper I wrote for my Feminist Theologies class. I rewrote Step Seven as, "We humbly and joyfully accepted our own empowerment." Looking back, I realize I am still seeking to balance the need to embrace my own power with the need to be humble.

How do I cultivate humility, while at the same time acknowledging my own empowerment?

13

When gossip, hate, and cruelty arise among friends or in public places, help me bravely walk forward with love. When I defensively assert certainty in the presence of the unknown, grant me the courage to live comfortably in the unanswerable questions of life.

—REV. STEPHEN M. SHICK

The humbling truth is that each one of us is capable of gossip, cruelty, and even hate. Each one of us can be a know-it-all when it comes to things we are passionate about or that we have a lot of experience with. Each one of us has acted in ways we would hate to have others witness and judge us for. Looking back on these behaviors, we feel powerless to change what we have done. And indeed, we can't.

To humbly face the truth of what we have done and probably will do again is a great learning experience. It is sometimes painful, and our shortcomings have so much to teach us. They can teach us how we would rather be with others. They can teach us how to keep a humble posture in our relationship to others. They show us how to treat others in the ways we want to be treated. They show us where we still need to grow.

How can I identify with those I judge harshly?

Finally, beloved, whatever is true, whatever is honorable, whatever is just, whatever is pure, whatever is pleasing, whatever is commendable, if there is any excellence and if there is anything worthy of praise, think about these things.

—PHILIPPIANS, 4:8

Humility takes loads and loads of practice. For years, I've been trying to cover up the things I don't like about myself by bragging or judging others or thinking my gifts of service were altruistic and had no redeeming function for myself.

Since acknowledging my flaws, practicing open-mindedness, and realizing that not only do I not know it all but no one does, I've been making progress toward becoming more humble. I am getting better at receiving criticism, which means both listening to it and not taking it too personally.

———

Am I open to learning new things today, realizing that humility takes practice?

15

*With humility, with awareness of the existence
of life, and of the sufferings that are going on
around us, let us practice the establishment of
peace in our hearts and on earth.*

—THICH NHAT HANH

This is one of the few quotes mentioning humility that I
could find in the primary Unitarian Universalist hymnal,
Singing the Living Tradition. The hymnal includes a topical
index of readings, listing topics from "acceptance of one
another" to "Yom Kippur," but there is no entry for "humility." Humility is not listed as one of the topics.

There is a multifaith and interspiritual website that I
often go to as a source of inspiration. It includes a guide to
thirty-seven universal spiritual practices, from "attention"
to "zeal." After "hospitality" comes "imagination." Humility
is not listed as one of the universal spiritual practices.

We are not alone in lacking humility in our lives. We are
not alone in our resistance to practicing humility. We are
not alone in our fear that we will misuse humility to pro-
mote low self-esteem. We are not alone.

With humility, we can be aware of the existence of life
beyond our own self-centeredness. With humility, we can
be aware that all suffer. We are not alone.

---

*How does practicing humility help me become
aware that I am not alone?*

It is unwise to be too sure of one's own wisdom.
It is healthy to be reminded that the strongest
might weaken and the wisest might err.

—MAHATMA GANDHI

I can remember holding an attitude of arrogance or, maybe more accurately, indifference. Someone might ask me a question, and rather than making a thoughtful reply, I was dismissive, or defensive, or didn't take time to try to understand what they were asking.

This still happens, but much more infrequently, and when it does, I am aware much sooner and am able to self-correct, making amends as soon as possible. I notice now that when I behave this way, it's usually because I'm overwhelmed, or stressed, or uncertain rather than wise.

As a corrective, I want to slow down, be more thoughtful in my answers, and not feel I have to have an answer for everything. One of the best things I can be is a lifelong learner. I may have wisdom, but it's good to remember that there is always new truth emerging.

Can I be sure of myself and still open to
continuing to learn?

17

When all is quiet and we are small and the night is dark, may we hear the tender breathing of all who lie awake with us in fear, that together we may gather strength to live with love, and kindness, and confidence.

—REV. JANE RANNEY RZEPKA

Each one of us lives with fear. Not one person can escape it. Whether large or small, fear is a part of being human.

One of the things we learn in Step Seven is to humbly and honestly ask a Higher Power to remove our defects of character. To turn over the fears we have experienced and the actions we have taken as a result of our fears. Not with the hope that we may live a life without fear entirely but with the intention that fear will not have the last word.

It is humbling to know that each human being on this earth struggles with fear. If you live with fear, welcome to the human race! It is good to have you with us.

This process of turning over our fears and our fear-driven behavior to something larger and more important than ourselves helps to keep fear in its rightful place, as one of the many emotions we experience on a daily basis. A signal that we might be in danger or that something isn't quite right. Not the primary driver of our thoughts and actions but rather just a feeling.

Where is fear running the show in my life today?

*Like the rest of us, I am a mixed grill of beauty
and self-centeredness, pettiness and magnanimity,
judgment and humility. On a bad day, I'm
pushing old ladies on the Titanic out of the way
to get to the lifeboats.*

—ANNE LAMOTT

Anne Lamott and her adult son are both in recovery. She tells the story of one day being at the peak of her anger with him. Stopping before she reacted violently to him, she realized this disease could kill her son—not that she would actually kill him but that the disease certainly could.

This disease could kill the beloved alcoholic in my life. This disease kills.

On a bad day, I sink into despair over the realization that this disease kills. On most days I find humor in what a "mixed grill" we all are. On good days, I remember that humility requires that I gaze into the eyes of my neighbor and look for our common story.

Humility reminds me that there will be good days and bad days. It also reminds me to develop my sense of humor and to remember that if I'm running around trying to push people out of my way, it might be time to be of service instead.

How does humor help me be humble?

19

*The attainment of greater humility
is the foundation principle of each of
AA's Twelve Steps.*

—BILL WILSON

When Bill Wilson wrote *The Twelve Steps and Twelve Traditions*, he defined humility as "the clear recognition of what and who we really are, followed by a sincere attempt to be what we can be."

Dictionaries define humility in many ways, but AA's definition includes "the desire to seek and do God's will."

This can be complicated for Unitarian Universalists, given our diversity of theology. But having an open mind as to the meaning of "God's will" has kept me sober. The theologian Paul Rasor reminds us that the symbol "God" offers a vision of our highest values and reminds us of our own human limitations.

I can use any word when I want to name the symbol that some name "God," but when I want to be reminded of the best, I call upon that Higher Power and remember that I am not it.

———

*What words can I use to name a vision
of the highest values of truth, justice,
love, and goodness?*

If we have any hope of transforming the world
*   and changing ourselves,*
we must be
bold enough to step into our discomfort,
brave enough to be clumsy there,
loving enough to forgive ourselves and others.

—REV. JOSEPH M. CHERRY

Continuing in the same comfortable patterns will get us the same results. To experience the change we hope for in recovery, we must be transformed. We end up changing and growing our hearts in a way that is both uncomfortable and deeply challenging. Feeling feelings is hard after we have spent a long time numbing ourselves.

And along the way, we recognize that there will be moments of missing the mark. To change, we must learn new things, new ways of being. What we have been trying on our own often does not work.

To embrace the change we want to see in our lives, we must be willing to say that we don't know exactly how to bring that change about. And then we surrender to the next right action, the next right thing, to move toward something larger: a power greater than ourselves, or the words and direction offered by someone who embodies the change we want to see for ourselves.

———————————

What change am I willing to embrace to move
toward deeper growth?

21

Humility is just as much the opposite of self-abasement as it is of self-exaltation. To be humble is not to make comparisons.

—DAG HAMMARSKJOLD

I once had a dream that I was sharing my workload with a colleague. In the dream I thought, "Oh, there's so-and-so, they are so much more skilled than I am." Even in my dreams I compare myself to others. It's so exhausting!

When you have raised a child to adulthood the world expects certain things. We join in the cocktail party of life, sharing how accomplished our children are. We don't start sentences with "My son the addict. My daughter the alcoholic." Instead, we find ourselves in social situations thinking, "Oh there's so-and-so, they are such a better parent than I am." It's so exhausting.

To be humble is not to make comparisons. To be humble is to recognize that we all have shortcomings, and the alcoholics in our lives are not our shortcomings. Imagine what it would be like to be humble and honest when someone asks, "And what does your offspring do?" Imagine telling the truth without apologizing for your parenting skills or praising yourself into martyrdom. Imagine being humble without making comparisons.

What does it look like for me to be honestly humble?

A person's pride will bring humiliation,
but one who is lowly in spirit will obtain honor.
—PROVERBS 29:23

Disruption and change are the new normal in our daily lives. In business, politics, nonprofits, and church, we're finding we can't do things the way we used to. We don't stay with the same company for our whole career, the incumbent doesn't always win, we work for systemic change, and many people no longer regularly attend religious services.

It used to be that I equated pride with strength. I thought I needed a strong ego to defend difficult work and bold decisions. The humiliation brought on by addiction stripped away from me my previous forceful behavior. These days, I think more, listen more, and remember to bring creativity to my daily life.

My ego is healthier when it's right-sized, not pride-filled.

———————

Have I examined my spirit to clear it of pride?

23

*Today, transcending boundaries is hard work.
For one thing, I've created more of them since I
was young. . . . For another thing, I'm much
more self-righteous and much less humble than
I was then.*

—Rev. Yvonne Seon

To identify with another beyond the fearful boundaries we erect is hard work. Our sense of self is challenged. We are no better than them: neither above nor below nor beyond.

These are pretty words, and much harder to practice in real life. It is hard to humble ourselves enough to say that we are not beyond doing the behavior that annoys us when someone else does it. At some point, the boundaries we have created hinder our connections to other human beings.

Today, just for today, let's be honest about where we have been self-righteous in putting ourselves above others. Let's acknowledge that the boundaries we put between "us" and "them" are a construct. Let's remember that we are continually learning how to connect again and again and again, never seeing the whole picture perfectly but continuing to try.

---

*What boundaries have I constructed between
myself and others? What might be needed
from me to tear them down?*

What's never questioned here is, whose standards of authenticity are being held up in the first place?
—ALOK VAID-MENON

As a queer person in Twelve-Step recovery, I often wondered if there was space for me in these rooms. Since the development of Al-Anon was based on the heterosexual marriage between Bill W. and Lois W., its literature and the people who participated often felt profoundly straight to me. I was scared at first to reveal the authenticity of my experience as an out, queer person.

And then, luckily, another person came into our Al-Anon meeting. She was around my age and she talked about her girlfriend who was down the hall in another Alcoholics Anonymous meeting. Just by listening to her share, I felt more comfortable there. Less alone. Able to really reveal the fullness of my experience in the rooms of recovery. It was such a gift to not feel alone.

We are here. We are queer. And though addiction is not always present in our LGBTQ community, for those of us who do struggle with addiction: we are in need of healing, and in need of healing in community. Our authenticity and our experiences are so very valuable to whoever is sitting in that chair next to us as we share. Perhaps, in showing up and being ourselves, we can help another person feel less alone.

How can I show up as my true, authentic self in relationships and in recovery?

25

If you want to go quickly, go alone.
If you want to go far, go together.
—African proverb

Poet Marge Piercy begins her poem "The Low Road" asking the question "What can they do to you?" The poem describes forms of possible physical abuse and then promotes all that can be done in community. It ends, "it starts when you say *We* / and know who you mean, and each / day you mean one more."

It's so easy to begin a project thinking I can do it myself. Committees and teams take too much time. They're so cumbersome. Everybody has a different way of doing things, another opinion and idea.

But we know that power and courage come from doing things together, from building community, from knowing that my idea alone does not bring about healthy change.

I love sitting in the back of the room, seeing all the wisdom that is in front of me, with me in the task of transformation. My courage comes from knowing I am not alone.

Who are my people? Have I checked in
with them recently?

I was the town cynic whose life was choked out
By a hidden disease of the heart
That I knew was there in my chest
But never told.

—JOSHUA LEACH

Criticism and judgment are two of the major character defects I live and have lived with. I am often critical of others out loud, though sometimes just silently in my head. The root of these thoughts is often "Well, they don't know what they're doing." Or even "I would do this better if I was in charge."

The gift of this recovery process has been recognizing that these thoughts come from deep fears and insecurities inside myself. I am afraid of how other people will see me. I am insecure about their judgments of me, so I am often quick to judge first. A fearful self-protection mechanism born out of being hurt by the words and actions of others.

I can't say I live my life completely free of judgment and criticism today. But what I can say is that I value connections with others so much more. I value these connections enough to risk the hurt that might come by living a more open and honest life with those I care about.

Where am I seeking to remain separate from
others? And where can I seek connection?

27

And the world cannot be discovered by a journey of miles, no matter how long, but only by a spiritual journey, a journey of one inch, very arduous and humbling and joyful, by which we arrive at the ground at our feet, and learn to be at home.

—WENDELL BERRY

Journey implies arrival. Each time I think I have arrived, I realize that arrivals are temporary. The ground at our feet is always shifting. Home is where I happen to be right now.

I once took a cross-country trip with the alcoholic in my life. It was a long, arduous journey. We stopped at the Grand Canyon. I worried they would wander off in the night. I don't know why I worried that; they had never done that sort of thing before. I worried they would be drunk and slip off the edge as I stood by helpless.

None of the things I worried about happened. We did all of the things one does at the Grand Canyon. We stayed long enough to watch the sunset, with the condors circling in the distance. We got as close to the edge as possible.

Usually, none of the things I worry about happen. I am humbled by what does happen. The unexpected moments of joy. The standing at the edge, looking over with awe.

What moments in my journey have humbled me and given me joy?

To learn which questions are unanswerable,
and not to answer them: this skill is most
needful in times of stress and darkness.

—URSULA K. LE GUIN

Sitting with uncertainty is deeply uncomfortable for me. I am someone who prizes knowledge and learning. I read a good number of books. I do what I can to be competent at work and in life.

The truth is that so much is unknowable. In human interaction, we know so little about the motives or the stories of others. In our universe, scientists constantly sit with the limits of their knowledge and where we find ourselves. In our daily lives, there are so many questions without answers in the midst of the tragic, the exciting, and the mundane.

This kind of discomfort used to lead me to use, so I could feel numb to it all. I didn't want to experience discomfort. But it also robbed me of living life with a full range of emotions, reactions, and resilience. Stress led me to the substance, not to curiosity about the discomfort or the ability to just sit with it. I am so grateful today that in the absence of using, I am able to embrace uncertainty better, to live in the in-between with more intention, to claim that there is so much I do not know and that is okay.

———

What can I sit with in my life that is unknowable?

Tidying is the act of confronting yourself.
—MARIE KONDO

On an airline flight I took some time to clean out my phone's photo stream. I actually discarded over two thousand pictures, many of them duplicates, and others that were taken for a specific time and place but had never been meant to stay on my phone taking up memory for years. Organizer Marie Kondo talks about how the act of discarding and organizing forces us to confront emotions about the past and anxiety about the future. And yet, when I am organizing, I am also confronted with my values and what matters to me most.

Confronting myself is not easy work, but the results are positive. It's not always easy to make a review of my day and admit when I am wrong, but it leads me to a more emotionally balanced life. My self-searching becomes a regular habit.

Each day, I want to not only do physical tidying but also to connect those tasks to the emotional tidying of my life. As tidying becomes a habit, my emotional as well as physical clutter diminishes, and I become more centered.

What do I have to tidy today?

He didn't mind how he looked to other people,
because the nursery magic had made him Real,
and when you are Real shabbiness doesn't matter.

—MARGERY WILLIAMS BIANCO

One of the deepest gifts of humility is facing the truth of who you are and being truly free to be that person, regardless of what others think. If we know our flaws and shortcomings, we no longer need to be obsessed with what others might say or think about us.

Ego tells us that we must manage our image and keep up appearances. That still keeps the focus on ourselves. And even if our self-image is very low, we are often attempting to manipulate others into thinking what we want them to think about us.

When we are able to see our whole selves, when we are able to dig down to the depths of our being, we are released from this kind of thinking. We are released to be in better relationship with others. We are released into authentic ways of being helpful to our communities. We are released from the thought-spiral that tells us we must appear one way or the other. We are free.

How can I embrace more of my shabbiness
in service of being Real?

31

*Kindness is more important than wisdom, and the
recognition of this is the beginning of wisdom.*

—THEODORE ISAAC RUBIN

Cheryl Strayed's book *Wild: From Lost to Found on the Pacific
Crest Trail* is the story of how the author hiked a trail that
runs from the Mexican to the Canadian border.

The story contains a lot about giving and generosity.
Strayed encounters a number of people on the trail and is
often wary at first. But almost always, these strangers are
exceedingly giving. After her boots accidently go flying over
a mountain ledge, some even help her fashion walking
shoes out of flip-flops and duct tape until she can find a new
pair of boots.

The book shows the unmitigated generosity of people, a
kind of humility, especially when they are joined together for
some common task. I think recovery can make people feel
that way too. In the "big book," Bill Wilson says, "We are
like the passengers of a great liner the moment after rescue
from shipwreck when camaraderie, joyousness and democracy pervade the vessel from steerage to Captain's table."

When I reflect on the struggles of my own life—including
the journey to sobriety—I am inspired to give to others, especially to those who have companioned me on my journey.

---

*How does reflecting on my journey inspire
service and generosity?*

August

STEP EIGHT: LOVE,

FORGIVENESS

Made a list of all persons we had

harmed and became willing to

make amends to them all.

I believe we can change the world if we start talking to one another again.

—MARGARET WHEATLEY

I believe that whatever we choose to call God or Love is most importantly about relationships. It's about our relationship to the unnameable and our relationships to all those we most love, and even those we just come across each day.

When my behavior was self-centered, I was only concerned about forgiveness that I felt others owed me, not about how I treated others. Getting clear about big mistakes I've made and making a list of people I've harmed is important work, because Love (or relationships) can return us to wholeness.

Social capital is transformational, but it doesn't happen if we isolate ourselves because we're too afraid to encounter those we've offended.

I have found that people are ready and waiting to forgive.

————————

Might I express love by having the courage to initiate an overdue conversation with someone I have offended?

Forgiveness is never easy, whether for yourself or someone else. Here is a place to forgive and to be forgiven.

—Cathy Cartwright-Chow

There was a long list of people I was not willing to forgive. In my Fourth Step process, I was invited to write down the name of each person and institution that I held a resentment against. The list was long. So long, I was almost ashamed to share it with someone else. Wasn't I supposed to be kind and loving? Isn't that what my Unitarian Universalist faith is all about?

As I reviewed a list of folks I held resentment against, as I reviewed a list of the people I had harmed, the person I was sharing with invited me into a spirit of forgiveness. She brought a great perspective on what I was responsible for and invited me to get clear about what I was not responsible for. Then she invited me to forgive others, either through making amends and taking responsibility for the harm I had caused or through prayer inside my own spirit and head.

Forgiveness is never easy, and it can be a slow process. It doesn't just happen overnight. I remember someone once telling me that forgiveness can only come when both parties can honestly own their part in the harm that was done. And in offering and receiving forgiveness, a burden was lifted. It felt easier to get sober and stick with sobriety without the weight of what I had done weighing on my shoulders.

———————

Where can I offer myself forgiveness and take responsibility for what I have done?

3

It is in pardoning that we are pardoned.

—Attributed to Saint Francis of Assisi

The most powerful and helpful teaching I ever heard about forgiveness was offered in a conversation with fellow spiritual directors. Our peer supervision group was discussing forgiveness. One of our number, a Catholic nun, said, "Sometimes it is not within our power to forgive. Forgiveness is an act of grace that God gives in God's time. But we can choose to be willing to forgive. Without that choice, forgiveness is not possible."

We don't have to believe in a personal God to see the logic of this teaching. Forgiveness is the freeing of the mind and heart from bearing the pain of a harm that someone has caused to us, and it can take a long time for that hurt to heal. But it will take much more time if we hold on to that hurt and replay it over and over. When we make a choice to be willing to forgive, trusting our Higher Power or our inner wholeness to do the work of healing, we help create the conditions for the freedom of forgiveness to happen. It may even be that we will wake up one day and discover that we have forgiven and are free.

Who have I not yet forgiven in my life, that I may now want to choose to be willing to forgive?

*If you haven't forgiven yourself something,
how can you forgive others?*

—DOLORES HUERTA

I often hear folx in recovery circles say, "You've been too easy on yourself all along. You've got to step up and become accountable."

While that may be true for some people, focusing on their past struggles is exactly what keeps some others from recovering from crippling dependence.

Dolores Huerta is famous for having co-founded the National Farm Workers Association, a precursor of the United Farm Workers, and for many other forms of advocacy and activism for agricultural laborers. She's been an inspiration to the whole state of California.

But she was criticized for her devotion to her work and the time she spent away from her children, and she struggled in the shadow of César Chávez. In order to be such an important leader, Huerta had to find forgiveness, for herself and others.

The powerful slogan "Sí, se puede" came from Dolores's lips. We can now repeat it because we understand forgiveness.

---

*How might I forgive myself today, while still
holding myself accountable?*

5

The work of forgiveness is so challenging—the actual work of it. The naming, grieving, empathizing, releasing. It's like a death. A death of what we wanted, what we expected, what we'd hoped for, what we deserved and didn't receive. . . . We don't get to control other people or outcomes. I am as devastated about this as you.

—JEN HATMAKER

Becoming ready to forgive has been one of the hardest parts of recovery for me. It is a complete release of all of the grudges I have held on to, all of the ways I have wanted to blame others for my life situation. The things I have held on to have been weighty. And they have been a bit of an excuse to live life a certain way, to treat other people a certain way, and to not take responsibility for the ways I have contributed to circumstances that have brought harm into my life and into the lives of others.

And letting all of this go is such a relief. To no longer hold on to the blame and shame directed at others has been a release. It took energy to hold all of that up, to keep the stories going in my head about how others were wrong. When I put the weight down, I was able to really own my part in it all and make my way toward a more solid recovery.

———————

Where have I been holding on to blame of others?

*Through our suffering and lack of forgiveness, we tend
to do all kinds of unskillful things that hurt others.
We close ourselves off from love . . . out of fear of
further pains or betrayals. This alone—a lack of
openness to the love shown to us—is a way that we
cause harm to our loved ones.*

—NOAH LEVINE

There is a three-part Buddhist practice that goes back to the time of the Buddha. First, bring to mind the face of a person you have harmed. Silently say to them words like this: "Please forgive me. For any ways that I have harmed you, in thought, or word, or deed, intentionally or unintentionally, please forgive me." Notice what feelings arise as you say this. Try to accept those thoughts and feelings without judgment.

After a time, bring to mind the face of a person who has harmed you. Silently say words like this: "I forgive you. For any way that you have harmed me, in thought, or word, or deed, intentionally or unintentionally, I forgive you." Again, simply notice the thoughts, feelings, and sensations that arise.

Finally, bring to mind a picture of yourself. Silently say words like this: "I forgive myself. For all the ways that I have harmed myself and others, in thought, or word, or deed, intentionally or intentionally, I forgive myself. For all the ways that I have harmed myself and others, out of fear, out of self-hatred, out of delusion, out of denial, I forgive myself."

———————

*Do I find this practice helpful? Does it bring my
heart peace?*

We made a list of all the persons we had harmed, and became willing to make amends to them all.

—STEP EIGHT

Franciscan friar Richard Rohr talks about Jesus' "higher economy of grace and mercy" but adds that it doesn't just replace the old, lower one of merit. "The universal principle is called 'transcend and include.' When you move to higher states of love and transformation, you do not jump over the earlier stages but must go back and rectify the earlier wrongs, or there will be no healing or open future for you—or for those you have hurt."

What this means to me is that I can't stop working on these Steps, learning this way of being. I must search my past behaviors, even the way I behaved last week.

Love and forgiveness, the themes for this month, go together. In order to keep on loving, forgiveness is a necessary action. Action means that my behavior needs to change, and I am responsible for making an apology and figuring out how I will do better.

Have I looked carefully at the list I made?
Are there people I have left off because I don't
think I owe them amends?

Blessed are they who make giant mistakes, whose intentions are good but impact has injured, who know the hot sense of regret and ask for mercy, for their hearts will know the gift of forgiveness.

—REV. ROBIN TANNER

The distinction between intention and impact is such a healthy tool for discerning who to make amends to. When reviewing the list of folks we have harmed, it's good to look at what the impact of the harm has been and hold that separate from our intention. Focusing on impact helps us to see where we have actually caused harm, without being distracted by judgments about our own character.

Looking at the list of those we have harmed through a lens of impact also helps us to see where we are taking on or owning harms that are not our own. If the harm did not come about through our actions but rather through the actions of others, we do not have amends to make. It can be hard for folks who grew up in alcoholic homes or who love others who live with addiction to know this, because we are used to owning all of the responsibility. There are some harms, however, that we cannot own because we didn't cause them.

In readying ourselves to ask for mercy and make amends, in becoming willing to approach others to own our harms, let us own the impact of our actions separate from our intention in doing them. And let's release that which is not ours to own.

When was a time this past week when my acts had a different impact from what I intended?

O Spirit of Love, enlarge our sympathies toward all troubled folk. Let us be generous of heart, that we might forgive and be forgiven.

—REV. RICHARD S. GILBERT

For the longest time, I believed that folks who had harmed me, folks who I held a grudge against, had really intended to ruin my life. It felt plain as day to me. Those folks had actively sought to do me harm. They knew exactly what they were doing, they were cold and calculating, they had bad motives or were on some kind of power trip.

It was hard for me to understand that perhaps these folks had been hurt too. Perhaps something had happened in their life that left them troubled, that was actually deserving of sympathy rather than my anger and resentment.

When I was thinking about all of the harm they intended to do to me, it was hard to see the ways I too had harmed others. Because I had. My actions had also harmed others. How could I avoid hurting others when I was so hurt myself?

May our hearts become large enough to see our own shortcomings in the ways we have treated others. May our hearts become large enough to extend sympathy to those who have hurt us. May our hearts become large enough to hold the complexity of the human spirit.

---

*Where have I been unwilling to see how
I have harmed another person?*

Finally, we begin to see that all people, including ourselves, are to some extent emotionally ill as well as frequently wrong, and then we approach true tolerance and see what real love of our fellows actually means.

—TWELVE STEPS AND TWELVE TRADITIONS

A phrase often heard at recovery meetings is "If you spot it, you've got it." This is akin to what Jesus taught when he said that we should first take the beam out of our own eye, before we take the sliver out of our neighbor's eye. If something bothers us about another person, there is a very good chance that they are exhibiting a trait or behavior that we ourselves possess but dislike and don't want to acknowledge. We are all flawed, all in need of tolerance and forgiveness.

Those of us in recovery don't have the luxury of blaming others for our problems. Resentments and self-pity are paths toward relapse. We only have the power to change our own behavior, to clean up our own side of the street. We cannot force others to think or behave as we would like them to. However, if we treat even those who vex and anger us with respect and kindness, our relationship with them has a good chance of changing for the better.

Do the people in my life who bring up dislike and anger in me exhibit any traits and behaviors that I dislike in myself?

11

Your child has fallen into the mire, and its body and its garments are defiled. You cleanse it, and array it in clean robes. The query is, Do you love your child because you have washed it? Or, Did you wash it because you loved it?

—Rev. Hosea Ballou

Love and forgiveness are entwined, like humans are mixtures of ingredients, and perfection is as problematic a concept as evil.

In recent years, I've been moved by learning of people who have forgiven a hate-filled person who came into their church with the intent to kill, and did so. Their response was complicated, including grief and a yearning for justice and security mixed with their theological statement of forgiveness. I can only guess what it would feel like to have a parent or a child murdered and then offer forgiveness soon afterward. I'm sure my grief would be all over the place, but I know I wouldn't want hatred to take over my life.

On most days, love and forgiveness are blended together, like when I wash my puppy because I love it. Forgiveness for its troublesomeness barely crosses my mind, because I know that dogs get dirty and it is my job to clean them up.

Where do I need a reminder today that love and forgiveness are entwined?

I wondered if I was worthy of love
But our faith kept loving me.
I found it impossible to forget
But our faith said, "Forgive yourself first."

—REV. MEGAN VISSER

Unitarian Universalism is a faith focused on love, but it often feels easier to extend that love to others rather than to ourselves. With love at the center of our Universalist heritage, it is a wonder that so many of us think of ourselves as unworthy of love. This love is for everyone, including us.

For those of us who grew up in homes with addiction or dysfunction, it was so hard to know we were loved. Our parents struggled to show their love, and, truthfully, were incapable of giving us love at many points in our lives. Growing up in this environment, we internalized that our lives did not matter and that we were inherently flawed.

Our call is to keep love at the center of our lives by acting compassionately toward ourselves and others. Our call is to consider our actions with a forgiving spirit, even and especially those that we cannot seem to shake or to forget. This is hard work. We cannot undo a lifetime's worth of messages in a few days, but we can begin with forgiving ourselves. We can take that deep breath and remind ourselves that we are beloved one day at a time.

Where is one place in my life where I can extend a
loving spirit?

Whatever words we utter should be chosen with care, for people will hear them and be influenced by them for good or ill.

—THE BUDDHA

When we think of all the harm that has been done because of careless speech, we are taken aback. Any sincere Eighth Step will reveal that many of the amends we owe are due because of careless speech.

The Buddha taught three criteria for judging whether something we say is right speech. The first is to ask ourselves, "Is it true?" This asks not only whether we are telling untruths with the intent to deceive. It also asks whether we are exaggerating to impress others or shading the truth to get out of our responsibility for a misstep.

The second question to ask ourselves is, "Is it helpful?" We have all suffered from the words of people who share unkind words that they think are true. We should be careful when being critical of others. When we spread unflattering gossip about people, we harm them in the eyes of others. Helpful speech is kind speech.

The third question to ask ourselves is, "Is this the right time?" Is the other person prepared to hear a truth we want to share, in this time and this place? Would it be better to wait? Or refrain altogether?

———

In what ways was my speech true, helpful, and timely? Were there any times when my speech was untrue, unhelpful, or untimely?

Each of us is more than the worst thing we've ever done.

—BRYAN STEVENSON

Lawyer and human rights activist Bryan Stevenson was shaped by the violent death of his elderly grandfather. After his death, which was caused by a young person, Stevenson's family didn't ask what kind of harsh punishment they wanted for the perpetrator but rather how had this happened? What has happened to us that young kids could stab an eighty-six-year-old man over a TV?

The fact that someone tells a lie once doesn't make them a liar by nature and forever. Trying to prevent an execution, Stevenson asked, "Why do we want to kill all the broken people? I realized, I represent broken people. Then I realized I sometimes work in broken systems. I do what I do because I am broken, too."

It takes a while, but when I finally realize I am broken too, then I can begin to be part of the solution. I can begin to heal.

Where does my brokenness become my asset?

15

There are two circumstances that lead to arrogance: one is when you're wrong and you can't face it; the other is when you're right and nobody else can face it.

—CRISS JAMI

Avoiding the pain of admitting we have harmed others can bring us to some pretty spiritually sick places. Time after time, we tell ourselves we were right about that person or that circumstance. Time after time, we dig ourselves into further shame and isolation. Not being willing to admit our harms brings deep anxiety, fear, rage, resentment, and so much more.

There are times when we have wanted to put ourselves above being hurt by others. Or we have wanted others to see the ways they have hurt us, expecting them to face this truth and own it. These expectations often led to disappointment, further hurt, and moments of denial or self-doubt.

At the turning point of Step Eight, we list out all those we have harmed, face the harms we have done, and become willing to begin the process of amending our behavior. It is a truth-telling, humble, and deep part of our recovery that can lead to healing beyond our wildest dreams. Being willing to own where we have been wrong puts us on the same level as everyone else, and the amends work we are preparing to do moves us toward healing.

When have I expected others to admit their wrongs while I was unwilling to admit my own fault?

We forgive ourselves and each other.
We begin again in love.

    —Rev. Robert Eller-Isaacs

It is so hard to forgive ourselves first or even to hold the things we have done in a forgiving spirit. To be able to forgive and to be fully forgiven comes with owning the entirety of the situation, which is the spiritual work we do in Step Eight. As we become willing to make amends, we also face the fullness of our actions and are given ways to own and release all that has transpired in our lives.

We also forgive others. We forgive them for our own benefit, for a release of all of the bad thoughts that have consumed our moments and days. We forgive them because we can hold on no more. Holding on to resentment and hate and jealousy does not benefit us, and it keeps us cut off from those around us as well as from our Higher Power.

Sometimes forgiveness comes in a letter that we read aloud to a sponsor or a trusted friend. Sometimes forgiveness comes in a prayer. Sometimes the forgiveness we need comes when we forgive ourselves, noticing that our resentment was less about them than about us. And there are times when forgiveness is gradual, where we wake up one day realizing we are no longer holding on to a grudge that used to ring in the back of our minds.

In forgiveness, we find peace with ourselves and with each other.

———

Where can I embrace forgiveness for myself?

17

Only the development of compassion and understanding for others can bring us the tranquility and happiness we all seek.

—The Dalai Lama

Those of us in recovery cannot afford to dwell in emotions that are harmful even to people without addictions. Self-pity, our "big book" says, is almost certain to lead to relapse if we indulge in it long enough. Blaming others for our problems and not taking responsibility for our own contributions corrodes our happiness and, eventually, our recovery. We can make little progress if we do not address and take care of our anger, our self-righteousness, and our conceitedness.

Working our program does more for us than help us to stop engaging in our addictions. The Twelve-Step program for spiritual awakening, if worked diligently and sincerely, provides us with a proven path to overcome these emotions that steal our happiness and corrode our humanity. By using the tools the program provides, we can "know a new freedom and a new happiness." As a result, our relationships improve. We see that others are doing the best they can, and we can meet them with compassion and understanding.

––––––––––

When have I indulged in self-pity, blame, judgment of others, and feelings of self-importance? When have I been able to relate to others with compassion and understanding?

Being deeply loved by someone gives you strength,
while loving someone deeply gives you courage.

—ESTHER HUERTAS

There was a time in my life when addictive behavior muffled my connection to love. Whether this behavior was genetically passed to me or triggered by trauma, its result left me thinking that although I was able to love, there was a wall keeping me from it. I craved love that I felt I couldn't get.

When I made a decision that I could no longer live with the use of alcohol, I had no idea that I would be saved from my lifelong struggle with love, both my need for it and my wall blocking it. But what happened was a slow, steady flow toward health, toward new behaviors that took down the wall and helped me see that a great love was with me all along.

I am now free to love fully and openly. I am now able to feel the strength of the love I receive.

Might I be able to focus my day on the
love I give? How?

19

I wondered if that was how forgiveness budded; not with the fanfare of epiphany, but with pain gathering its things, packing up, and slipping away unannounced in the middle of the night.

—KHALED HOSSEINI

To begin a process of forgiving and being forgiven is often painful. It means facing the pain of harm we have caused and harm we have received. Sometimes this means breaking through denial. Other times it means slowly learning more and more about the reality of what has happened to us or what we have caused.

And this pain does not have to last forever. Whether we make moves toward amends or we begin the spiritual healing work we need to do to forgive, there is a way forward. We learn to live with the truth of what we have done to others. And we learn to live with the truth of what has been done to us.

Recovery invites us into balance, so we need no longer run from our past actions. Instead, we learn to face the truth of our lives and stay in it, rather than shrinking away.

Where have I been avoiding the pain of offering forgiveness or receiving forgiveness?

Forgiveness does not mean condoning or agreeing with a horrendous act. It is a decision to no longer attack one's self.

—GERALD G. JAMPOLSKY

One of the most common misunderstandings of forgiveness is the idea that it is something we do for the other person, most often someone who does not deserve it. But forgiveness is both simpler and much more complicated than that. Forgiveness is something we do for ourselves and not for the other person. There is a difference between forgiveness and reconciliation. We have achieved forgiveness when the harm that others have done no longer disturbs our peace with feelings of rage, resentment, and self-pity.

We can let others back into our hearts without necessarily letting them back into our lives. We have a right to protect ourselves when we can from others who would repeatedly harm us. When forgiveness is complete and we are at peace, we can then decide if we can be reconciled with the person and rebuild the relationship. And forgiveness requires that we see the other person as whole and not just through the lens of the ways they have harmed us.

Are there people I have forgiven that I want to be reconciled with? Am I at peace with the fact that there are others in my life that I can forgive but do not want to be in relationship with any longer?

21

We're all a little weird. And life is a little weird. And when we find someone whose weirdness is compatible with ours, we join up with them and fall into mutually satisfying weirdness—and call it love—true love.

—Rev. Robert Fulghum

In the rooms of recovery I have been in, where wisdom is abundant, there are informal reminders of many kinds. One is that when first entering recovery from addiction, when first making a decision to do things differently, one should not make other changes at the same time.

This can feel counterintuitive when, on a pink cloud of seeing a new world, I want to change everything. I want to move, change my job, buy a car, and get into a new relationship. Love seems everywhere around me and I want to be a part of it. I'm meeting people who are saying new things, doing things that seem healthier, and I want to connect!

I have found it's better to follow the common suggestion to first simply get a plant and see if I can keep it alive. Can I be in a relationship with that plant, day after day, even when it seems like nothing much is happening?

After a year or so, when the glow has softened, then it might be wise to make other changes. Love will follow when it's ready.

To what small thing can I show love today?

We gather together to face ourselves honestly, to forgive ourselves gently, to love one another fervently.

—Philip Larson

It often seemed like life was more exciting when I was using. There was so much going on! I was unpredictable. Life was unpredictable. I never knew who was going to show up and what state of mind they might be in. There were parties and moments of dancing, times I don't think I'll write about here, but take my word that life was thrilling.

And recovery was hard. It wasn't fun or thrilling. There were times when it was painful, when it felt repetitive and boring, when I felt emotions I wasn't interested in feeling, if I'm being honest. Folks want to tell us it is worth it to get into recovery, and they are right. And it's also hard and takes a good deal of work.

So now I look at what my life has become. I am a little more predictable and I party a bit less. But the joy I feel runs so very deep. The love I hold for the people in my life is more abundant than I ever could have imagined. The love I receive is incredible, and I feel it down to my core. I no longer find myself seeking excitement elsewhere, but more and more wanting to stay in the moment, to be present to what is right in front of me. What a gift.

What contentment is there to be found in the present moment?

23

We know in our deepest heart of hearts that unconditional love is somehow more true—more fundamental, more real, more radical (at the root)—than hate, which always seems to be confused, deluded, reactive, divisive and false. Love breeds love, and hate breeds hate. We all experience this.

—JOAN TOLLIFSON

It is wonderful that we always have a choice. It is also a heavy responsibility. In every moment, we have a choice to manifest love—attention, acceptance, compassion, and caring—or its opposites, hate and judgment. We can always choose love, if we resolve to be conscious of what we are doing.

All of us imperfect humans, particularly those of us who are in recovery, act out of fear, hate, and judgment from time to time. The cultivation of love is a lifelong project. The good news is we have the tools to do that—in working the Steps, in the companionship of people with wisdom and good sobriety, and in our spiritual practices. And when we slip, we simply start over. In time, the fruits of acting from love will be firmly established in our minds and souls. And, having experienced how much it hurts to push anyone or anything out of our hearts, we will turn ever more naturally toward love.

―――――――――

When I pay attention to my decisions to speak or act, do I find that I am intending to act out of love or out of fear and judgment?

A heart still works even when it's broken.
—CHARLES BLOW

One of my siblings and I often reflect on our childhood, the differing traumas we experienced, and how we are trying to heal from them now. One of us felt the sting of abuse from our dad, the other of neglect from our mother. Addiction had been present in various ways in our parents' childhoods, and I felt it being passed down.

As a result, not only was I wounded but I also began to wound others in my life. The work I am charged to do now asks me to take a look at all those I have harmed and become willing to make amends. Sometimes, even after doing this work for years, I find that I still get stuck because of my broken heart. I lash out at others when what I really want to do is clear away all the debris I have created.

Our parents are no longer living. My siblings and I are the generation that can make change. Part of committing to my recovery is applying myself to heal my heart. My heart has been broken, but it is healing. I am becoming stronger as I work on forgiveness in my present.

———

*Can I take my broken heart and be willing
to mend the hurts I have caused?*

25

*Forgiveness is the name of love practiced among
people who love poorly. The hard truth is that
all people love poorly. We need to forgive and
be forgiven every day, every hour increasingly.*

—FR. HENRI NOUWEN

I know I have had moments of loving others poorly. Times
when I did not honor the other person's dignity. Times when
I got angry and raged. Times when I gossiped and spread
rumors. This poor behavior often happened while I was
attempting to love, to hold someone dear, to make sense of
what it meant to be in a relationship.

To become willing to make amends, I had to begin by
thoroughly searching my heart for the harms I had caused.
I also had to remain open to the fact that I did not have the
entire picture—that people I had loved and cared for also held
the truth of their experience. A part of becoming willing to
make amends was becoming willing to hear that truth.

Not one of us loves perfectly all the time. In fact, I agree
that all of us love poorly on a regular basis. We are human.
So what we can do is become willing to face the ways we
have loved poorly and to listen to those we have loved as we
learn more about the forgiveness and amends we seek.

What is one way I have loved poorly?

*Try to see the good in others. When you're
tempted to judge someone, make an effort to see
their goodness. Your willingness to look for the best
in people will subconsciously bring it forth.*

—MARIANNE WILLIAMSON

We contract our hearts and souls when we judge others.
We also unleash a lot of unhealthy reactions in our bodies.
Judging others is unhealthy from the perspectives of body,
mind, spirit, and recovery. Just as important, when we judge,
we distort our perceptions of reality. We don't see the other
person the way they are, in all their complex humanity.
They are complex as we are complex and flawed as we too
are flawed. Subtly or obviously, the distortion of judgment
influences our relationship to the other person and brings
harm to both parties.

Like any bad habit, the habit of judgment requires time,
awareness, and compassion—compassion for the other
person and for yourself—in order to change. It hurts to put
another person out of your heart. Our Twelve-Step program is designed to give us ways to change that habit, and
part of the program is the Seventh Step: prayer to our Higher
Power to remove all of our shortcomings. As we work our
Steps, attend meetings, and pray for those we resent, we can
know the freedom of a life that is increasingly free of judging others.

---

*Have I asked my Higher Power to remove
my tendency to judge others?*

27

Throughout life people will make you mad,
disrespect you and treat you bad.
Let God deal with the things they do,
'cause hate in your heart will consume you too.

—WILL SMITH

Early on in recovery, I was fixated on what people had done to me, both in my childhood and in my recent past. So, whenever I was obsessed with someone or something they had done, I went to this passage in the "big book":

> If you have a resentment you want to be free of, if you will pray for the person or thing that you resent, you will be free. If you will ask in prayer for everything you want for yourself to be given to them, you will be free.... Even when you don't really want it for them and your prayers are only words and you don't mean it, go ahead and do it anyway. Do it every day for two weeks, and you will find you have come to mean it and to want it for them, and you will realize that where you used to feel bitterness and resentment and hatred, you now feel compassionate understanding and love.

Suddenly, as ridiculous as it felt, I began to focus on the prayer, about the hopeful things *I* wanted. I began to focus on not missing a day, lest I have to start over and do another two weeks. Not only did it work, but the compassion I began to feel widened to include myself.

Am I obsessed with the poor treatment I have
received from someone?

And so on this day we pray for those things we struggle with. For the conflicts we feel within ourselves and between us and those we love. We pray for guidance, compassion, for the opening of a path.

—REV. KRISTA TAVES

Early on in recovery, I heard the invitation to pray for those with whom I was in conflict, even for those whom I hated. I wondered what the benefit was, but my sponsor and those around me encouraged me to do it and so I did it.

At first, it felt forced. Like I was just doing something because I should, not because I really meant it. I prayed for this person whom I spent most of my days mad at. And my early prayers had that sort of tone—like I was angrily saying these prayers between my teeth for their well-being and their healing.

And then the day arrived when I realized my heart had softened. I was no longer attached to the negative outcomes I had wanted for this person and their life circumstances. I was not praying angrily but genuinely for their well-being and healing. It did not necessarily change our relationship, but something in me changed. I was willing to let go of much that I had been hanging on to with this person.

We never got to a place of resolution or healing between us. There was no happy ending. But I can say with confidence today that I wish for their healing and well-being, something that seemed impossible at one time.

Whose healing and well-being do I need to pray for?

29

If you have a resentment you want to be free of,
if you will pray for the person or thing that you resent,
you will be free.

—*ALCOHOLICS ANONYMOUS,*
"THE BIG BOOK"

Sometimes we need to act our way into being. As we hear in the rooms of those in recovery, "Fake it till you make it." You may be skeptical at first, but if you are in a difficult relationship with someone else or in conflict with them, pray for them for two weeks. You will be surprised at how much that changes your behavior and your attitude about the situation. Just say the words. It doesn't matter that you don't mean them at first. Saying the words shows a willingness that is deeper than the conscious will and is part of the surrender to our Higher Power that is necessary to achieving and maintaining recovery.

Pray that they will be happy. Pray that they will be safe from harm. Pray for their health. Pray for their burdens to be eased. Your conscious will may resist, but remember that it is the self-centered assertions of our will that have led us into the addictions from which we seek recovery. Praying for our enemies is a step in the all-important surrender we need to make in order to be free. We need to surrender to the Steps, the group, and our Higher Power. And we will know a new freedom and a new happiness.

———

Can I pick one person with whom I am having
difficulty and pray for them every day for two weeks?

30

Resentment is like a poison we carry around inside us with the hope that when we get the chance we can deposit it where it will harm another who has injured us. The fact is that we carry this poison at extreme risk to ourselves.

—BERT GHEZZI

In her book *The Best Awful*, Carrie Fisher included a saying common in AA meetings: "Resentment is like drinking a poison and then waiting for the other person to die."

The saying has become so common that people outside of recovery use it a lot, with diverse attributions, because its absurdity and element of truth always get a chuckle. The laughter is designed to break down the defenses of the person who is talking about their resentment.

The point that Ghezzi's phrasing makes especially clear is that we are carrying around this poison, thinking that we are waiting to use it on someone else, when it is already killing us slowly.

To be able to be aware of resentment is crucial, so that it does not linger with us, simply waiting for a moment when it can take effect. Daily attention to our spiritual fitness brings love and acceptance to the fore and dries up resentment.

———

What actions have I taken today to address my spiritual fitness?

31

When you fight with reality, you lose.
But only 100% of the time.

—BYRON KATIE

"Expectations are resentments under construction" is a phrase often spoken in Twelve-Step meetings. Addicts and alcoholics cannot afford to have resentments if we want to maintain our recovery. There is so much useless suffering in the world caused by the belief that others should change and that others should act differently. But we have no power over the choices others make, and so our expectations of others make little sense. What we do have power over are our own feelings, reactions, and actions. Which brings us to another phrase often uttered in meetings and by sponsors: "You can only clean up your own side of the street."

The Twelve-Step methods give us the tools we need to do that. We can pray for the people we have difficulty with. We can remember the counsel of the Serenity Prayer. Is there anything you can change? Yes, your own attitude! We can talk with our sponsor. We can try to let go of worry and anger and just do the next right thing, leaving the rest to our Higher Power.

Relationships are like a dance. When one partner changes the steps, the other person responds in some way. And you would be surprised how often that response improves the situation.

What do I need to do to clean up my own side
of the street in a troubled relationship?

September

Made direct amends to such people
wherever possible, except when to
do so would injure them or others.

SEPTEMBER

If merely "feeling good" could decide, drunkenness would be the supremely valid human experience.

—WILLIAM JAMES

When I was young, I struggled with feeling good enough about myself. I took the criticism I received to heart. When I came into recovery, what I most had to confront was how I had been diminishing myself for so many years. Rather than ignoring my flaws, my ego was all wrapped up in self-criticism. I turned to alcohol as a false way to make myself feel better.

While I appreciated the importance of Twelve-Step work, I found it helpful to read additional recovery materials designed for my own gender identity, as well as materials written from a Buddhist perspective. I have supplemented my program with therapy and made sure that I engaged with other spiritual practices.

Years into recovery, I've kept up my important Twelve-Step work. I have forgiven my own struggles with unworthiness, and I also forgive the original Twelve-Step founders for focusing on only one segment of the population. Most importantly, I don't need alcohol to feel good.

When do I feel truly good?

We all know loss and pain.
Let none of it divide us.
In the rising sun today
Let us do together what we cannot do alone:
Roll away the stones that close our hearts.

—Rev. Joel Miller

Resentments and fears can feel like stones that close our hearts. We hang on to them. The stories we return to over and over again. The ways we have been wronged. And even deeper, the fears. Fear of being found out for a fraud. Fear that we are not enough. Fear of things not going our way. These are stones that close our hearts, keep us disconnected, foster isolation.

The process of recovery asks us to make amends, to own the ways our resentments and fears and our character defects have caused harm to others. We have been selfish. We have had our own part in the resentments we hold, even if only by hanging on to them. Deciding to roll these stones away can be terrifying. It is also a truthful process that has the power to set us free.

This is a process we cannot go through alone. There are folks helping us along the way—sponsors, friends in recovery, our ministers—who can offer guidance and give us space to roll away those stones, that we may live a life that is freer and less tethered to the past.

What stones are closing my heart?

3

Compassionate people ask for what they need.
They say no when they need to, and when they say
yes, they mean it. They're compassionate because
their boundaries keep them out of resentment.

—BRENÉ BROWN

During my days of drinking, my experience with setting boundaries took two basic forms. One: I would set a boundary and then feel guilty about having said "no" and feel concerned that perhaps the person would not like me because I said "no." Two: I would fail to set and maintain a boundary, saying "yes" when I wanted to say "no," and feel resentful of the person whom I held responsible for the violation I had permitted.

I now realize that a big part of the start of my alcohol overuse involved my inability to set and maintain healthy boundaries. I am an introvert by nature and, in high school and college especially, it seemed that social events and social groups were the measure of a person. I found that alcohol allowed me to pose as an extrovert, despite the fact that the behavior was uncomfortable for me and left me feeling drained. Accepting what I need as an introvert requires that I say "no" to the gathering after the event because I need this time to decompress in solitude.

It takes courage to set boundaries and enforce them.

———————

Do I let my fear of being unpopular stand in the way of
my setting and maintaining healthy boundaries, or do I
state and maintain these boundaries gently yet firmly?

Courage is the most important of all the virtues because without courage, you can't practice any other virtue consistently.

—MAYA ANGELOU

My Unitarian ancestor William Ellery Channing spoke of the difference between understanding courage as "an instinct bordering on rashness" and seeing it as the "wise moral judgment" that can make a difference in one's own life and the life of others.

Senator John McCain exemplified, and also wrote about, this quality. He wrote, "If you do the things you think you cannot do, you'll feel your resistance, your hope, your dignity, and your courage grow stronger. . . . You will someday face harder choices that very well might require more courage. . . . And when those moments come . . . and you choose well, your courage will be recognized by those who matter most to you."

The courage we need today may not be as profound as that of a prisoner of war or someone starting a new faith. But each small thing we do may lead to the next and begin to give us strength to repair the past and make the future one with meaning.

What small thing that I've been ignoring needs a dose of courage?

5

I put my faith in you.
I put my faith in every one of you who woke up this
morning with the weight of loss—manifesting as
numbness, anger, fear, or an alienating, aching pain.

—Rev. Anya Sammler-Michael

Recovery is a very human endeavor. Each one of us who has been touched by addiction has been hurt, and we have hurt others. In Step Nine, we acknowledge those hurts to the people we have harmed, and we offer to do what we can to make them right.

It is difficult, when we are feeling hurt or angry or numb, to go to another to acknowledge what we have done to them. People often suggest praying for those we make amends to before approaching them, so that we may have time for our hearts to soften and for the hard edge of our resentments and fears to become just a bit more flexible. Still, this is deep spiritual work, and it is very human work.

In taking Step Nine, we place our faith in something larger than ourselves to carry us through the process. We also place our faith in the person we are making amends to, trusting that we will be heard and trusting that this person will be honest and authentic in their response. Two human beings coming together in the midst of so much. What a sacred endeavor and practice.

Who shall I put my faith in today?

No man, for any considerable period, can wear
one face to himself and another to the multitude,
without finally getting bewildered as to which
may be the true.

—NATHANIEL HAWTHORNE

My addictive behavior caused me to wrap myself in a smothering cloak of inauthenticity. I altered my consciousness so that I could feel like someone else, so I could appear to be someone else, and ultimately I became so lost in the deceptions that I did not recognize the person I had become.

At first alcohol allowed me to feel less anxious. Then it allowed me to appear more carefree and bold. My dishonesty about how much I drank led to dishonesty about when and where I drank. Honesty was the first principle to fall. Integrity and compassion soon followed.

Authenticity requires courage because honesty and transparency make us vulnerable. At the same time, that vulnerability allows us to maintain the healthy connectedness that is the opposite of addiction.

———————

Am I doing all that I can to muster the courage to be
authentic and to embrace the resulting vulnerability
as my path to forming healthy connections and
avoiding unhealthy ones?

We need to get messy. We need to question our assumptions about who makes a good fit, and why we think people are puzzle pieces that have to slide into the existing system.

—Rev. Matthew Johnson

When I first entered recovery, I felt like my problem was that I was really "messy," and what I needed was to tidy up, to get my act together. My life was out of control. But that's a different kind of mess from the kind in which I realize the complexity of Unitarian Universalism and the assumptions I have made about who belongs in it.

Years ago, I didn't think that people with addictions fit into this faith. But we do. And I didn't think that people of this faith could participate in Twelve-Step programs, because the programs' spirituality was not the same as ours. But that was wrong, too.

We may be puzzle pieces, but our puzzle is bigger and more complex than I originally understood. Who we are is as diverse as we say our faith is, both theologically and otherwise.

Now I have courage to be who I am and to get messy in a new way.

Where can I get messy in my faith or spiritual tradition?

*Do not fear agitation, for agitation is the rhythm of
    life itself; to be put into motion, to be stirred.*
*Do not fear the movements that decenter what you
    always thought permanent.*
*You carry within the center of your understanding,
    the compass to show you the way.*

—Rev. Tania Márquez

Coming into Step Nine, I had so much fear about what would be revealed about me. Faced with going to others to make amends and own the harm I had caused, I imagined each one of them telling me, "You are the worst." And it was a bit disconcerting. It brought to front and center what I thought about myself and what I had projected onto others.

In the process of making amends, however, things turned out differently than I had imagined. It was a time to decenter my own needs and to hear out the other person—to center the harm they had experienced rather than making the encounter all about me.

What I can tell you is that this process of making amends transformed my life. It gave me courage to face what I had done. It gave the people I had harmed the opportunity to be heard and honored, and, if desired, it allowed a relationship to blossom anew. The healing for both parties and the sense of being heard and honored allowed space for compassion to emerge.

---

*Where can I decenter my own needs today
to be helpful to another?*

*You can learn new things at any time in
your life if you're willing to be a beginner.
If you actually learn to like being a beginner,
the whole world opens up to you.*

—BARBARA SHER

In my career, I learned to question everything. I had been in my narrow field for some time, so I was accepted as being knowledgeable. It was very difficult for me to take advice from others. It was difficult to accept that I had used alcohol to alter my perception and my reasoning capability such that, for at least a couple of years, acting on extreme or sudden ideas of my own was probably not a good idea.

It requires considerable courage, especially in early recovery, to listen to advice from others. We may recall having been capable, and perhaps exceptional, at rational thinking and problem solving before we lost control of our ineffective coping mechanism. It is very difficult to accept that prolonged or intense addictive behavior can alter mental capacity.

"Beginner mind" is a Zen Buddhist term that describes the willingness to approach new experiences and new ways of thinking and remain aware that our own thinking may be biased.

---

*Am I willing to approach life with a
"beginner mind"?*

Be bold and mighty forces will come to your aid.
    —JOHANN WOLFGANG VON GOETHE

I have learned, in my time in recovery from abusing substances, that boldness no longer means recklessness. I used to think being bold meant behaving like a bull in a china shop, and that the attention I drew made me a leader. That was foolish thinking, fueled by addiction.

Now, boldness means not giving up from doing something hard. It means not covering up difficult situations because they're tough to look at.

Boldness means facing my feelings rather than ignoring them. When I have amends to make to another, I try to be bold in reflection and then prudent when determining when to approach or when it may be wise to hold back.

I am never alone in doing this work. I have a Higher Power, and I have connections with others in recovery who are always there to support me. By availing myself of the support of others, I am held.

Am I connected to my sources of strength
so that I may face this day?

11

There is, finally, only one thing required of us: that is, to take life whole, the sunlight and shadows together; to live the life that is given us with courage and humor and truth.

—REV. KENDYL R. GIBBONS

To get into recovery requires courage. Courage to honestly face the things we have done. Courage to admit that we have a problem and are in need of help. Courage to continue asking for help, especially in those moments when we feel we least need it. Courage to accept the life that has been given us and what we are called to do with that life.

And there will be times when we fall short of this courage. Times when our fears get the best of us. Times when the addiction feels so strong and we feel ever so powerless to face it. We cannot all be courageous all of the time. And we certainly cannot be courageous entirely on our own.

In moments of struggle, the real courage comes when we reach out to tell someone. The courage shows up when we stop fighting with whether or not we are suffering. It comes to us when we accept our difficult times and we reach out to someone to share, to feel less alone, and to be on the receiving end of some help.

Let's take courage today, dear friends, and take the next right action toward our recovery.

Where am I being called to show up courageously?

We need quiet time to examine our lives openly and honestly—spending quiet time alone gives your mind an opportunity to renew itself and create order.

—SUSAN L. TAYLOR

During the final days of my addictive behavior I found it unbearable to be still while sober or to be alone while sober. After some time in recovery, I realized that it is solitude that allows me to identify what is coming from inside me: What am I thinking? What am I feeling?

Running from ourselves allows us to maintain the delusion that there is no problem with the addictive behaviors that are in fact consuming us. We can manically avoid stillness and solitude until we completely drown out the voice inside that is crying out, fully aware that something is horribly amiss.

Solitude requires courage because it is in solitude that we are no longer distracted from ourselves.

Am I gently developing the courage to explore solitude and teaching myself to stop running from myself?

13

By choosing integrity, I become more whole, but wholeness does not mean perfection. It means becoming more real by acknowledging the whole of who I am.

—PARKER J. PALMER

Today I will acknowledge the whole of who I am. Far from a wallow in self-pity that leads to unhealthy behavior, my acknowledgment of my whole self is a new beginning of improvement.

Whatever my flaws, seeing them with honesty can help me to face the day, and as I accomplish needed tasks, I am not overwhelmed with fear. Sometimes, I need to repeat "One thing at a time" to remind myself that I can't accomplish everything all at once.

At the end of the day, I am able to review that day's behavior, and sleep comes easily.

I become more whole.

Can acknowledging the whole of who I am, good and bad, help me today?

*We are not perfect, but we are perfectly fitted for
    this day.
We are not without fault,
but we can be honest to face our past as we chart
    a new future.*

> —REV. KIMBERLY QUINN JOHNSON

None of us reading this right now is without fault. Each one of us has done things we would rather not talk about. We strive to do the best we can, and sometimes we fall short, hurting others because we are trying to get our own needs met in the wrong way.

Step Nine is all about honesty in facing our past. We make amends to people to clear up the damage we have done in others' lives up to this moment. The honesty and acceptance we embrace and receive in the Ninth Step are deeply healing, even if the process does not go perfectly how we planned. To own with others where we have hurt them and to remain open to making it right is one of the most honest actions we can take.

We take this Step because we cannot move forward into a different kind of future with the past hanging over our heads. We take this Step because we don't want to keep drinking or eating or gambling or compulsively acting out in response to our guilt or shame anymore. We take this Step because it helps us to accept that we are not perfect, we are not above being human.

---

*Where have I struggled to be honest, and what is
holding me back?*

15

There is one advantage to realizing that you're never going to get it right: you do begin to stop expecting everyone else to get it right too, which makes for less frustration when other people turn out to be just as human as you are.

—JEFF WILSON

Many of my decisions to drink involved lamenting my imperfections and drowning the pain of my mistakes. Many of my drunken episodes involved imagining my perfection, drowning the memory of my mistakes, and lamenting aloud the mistakes of others. I caused myself such misery trying to be perfect. I caused others such misery pretending to be perfect.

In recovery, I began to realize that my emotions are directly related to my beliefs, and I cause my own misery by clinging to beliefs that have no basis in reality.

We strive for perfection in ourselves and search for imperfection in others. We imagine perfection in others and loathe the imperfection we see in ourselves. Both these activities ensure that we will be unhappy, because we are not perfect and neither is anyone else.

The strength inherent in true courage allows us to be less judgmental of ourselves and others.

Am I being gentle with myself and others and accepting that perfection in human endeavors is imaginary?

There's really no such thing as the "voiceless."
There are only the deliberately silenced, or the
preferably unheard.

—ARUNDHATI ROY

In recent years society has developed a greater awareness of the silencing of marginalized communities, of oppressive structures that are designed to keep that society functioning in the status quo.

There are places in my life where I, too, felt silenced and unheard. I can now see that in the life I led before entering recovery I was good at not hearing others, because I was so focused on myself. And that focus was a big cup of self-pity in which I wallowed.

Now I am able to use my voice with more clarity, both to make amends to those I have hurt in the past, trampling on their agency, and to better express my own needs.

To whom do I owe amends for having
shown them disregard?

What have we got to lose?
A poverty of the spirit?
The lie that we are alone?

—Rev. Leslie Ahuvah Fails

Solitude has been a regular part of my life, first out of necessity and now out of choice. Growing up, I felt alone a lot. In my own home, I felt lonely and isolated often. When I was having feelings, the common response was "Go up to your room." When my alcoholic parent was in a rage, I felt like all I could do was bear it alone. For a time, being alone felt safe. At least I wasn't a burden to others, and I might not face the consequences of making someone else mad.

And then came the recovery. Then came the recognition that my childhood and my response to it were common. Then came the talking about it all instead of bottling it up inside. And I found I wanted to be in relationship with others. Letting other people in felt good. This change didn't happen overnight, it took time.

Now I would say that I still love my alone time, but not out of a sense of safety and protection. I want to be alone to recharge, to rest myself and renew my spirit. I no longer feel that loneliness, so I embrace moments of being alone. And I never thought this could be possible for me—never thought this would be my life.

Where can I embrace moments of alone time
to rest and renew my spirit?

18

In our instinctive attachments, our fear of change, and our wish for certainty and permanence, we may undercut the impermanence which is our greatest strength, our most fundamental identity. Without impermanence, there is no process. The nature of life is change. All hope is based on process.

—RACHEL NAOMI REMEN

I drank mostly from fear. The fear was often either that something would last or that something would not last. I feared that when good things happened I would not be able to maintain them, so I altered my consciousness with alcohol in attempts to extend my good feelings. I feared that bad things would never end, so I altered my consciousness with alcohol to withstand them.

Embracing impermanence allows us the courage to love something or someone with less fear of losing them. Embracing impermanence allows us the courage to withstand discomfort with less fear that it will never end.

Impermanence frightens us because it reminds us again of our vulnerability to things outside our control. Courage is required to focus on the realization that impermanence is the truth that makes pleasant things precious and unpleasant things bearable.

———————

Am I courageously embracing impermanence with the realization that impermanence is the truth that makes pleasant things precious and unpleasant things bearable?

19

All happiness depends on courage and work.
—HONORÉ DE BALZAC

There is a sentimental idea, a kind of wishful thinking, that happiness is the absence of responsibility or care. True happiness can be equated with serenity, with having right relationship with oneself and the world.

When I am engaged with the Ninth Step, being willing to make amends to those I have hurt, it is work. Sometimes it's easier than other times, but it takes a certain level of courage to engage in making things right.

Once that wreckage of my past is cleared up, I can stay vigilant on a daily basis so that I create less of a mess. This is still work, even when what I'm engaging in is emotional and spiritual work.

Am I willing to engage in courageous
personal work today?

*At times we may fear that love will not be strong
    enough.*
*At times we may question whether love really is
    at the root of all things,*
*in this world with so much struggle and suffering
    and discord.*

—Rev. Laura Horton-Ludwig

To make amends to another person is to trust in a larger love holding you both. It is a beautiful act of love to be able to come forward and admit our wrongdoing.

These conversations and the actions that follow can heal relationships long torn apart. They can bring us into alignment with a larger will. And when we seek to repair harm, our actions affect not just the folks who are involved but also ripple out into every interaction that they have from then on. Maybe we end up treating others who have wronged us more compassionately. Maybe we end up holding others accountable when we used to tolerate behavior and actions that did not honor our worth.

There is a larger love holding us when we get honest and earnestly seek to heal our past. There is a larger love holding us when we clean up our side of the street and let go of the expectation that others must do exactly what we are doing. There is a larger love holding us when we just reach out to see what might be possible between us, our communities, and our world.

———————

Where can I trust in a larger love holding me?

21

You got to be right with yourself before you can be right with anybody else.

—August Wilson

So many times have I felt afraid to share my story, fearing rejection for the mistakes I have made in my life. Yet what I recall from each time I have risked vulnerability to share with others how I have struggled are the positive and encouraging responses. I recall the times when others have thanked me for saying what they needed to hear. I recall the times others have stated that hearing my journey gave them hope for themselves or their loved ones. I remember the times when others immediately admitted to their own struggles and took that all-important first step of asking for help they had been too ashamed to request before.

I need to remind myself that, for my own growth journey and to assist others along their paths, I need to have the courage to risk negative responses, born from fear and misunderstanding, in order to experience those transformational responses that help others and sustain me in the work I am called to do.

———————

Am I waiting until I feel more courageous to do the things that frighten me, or am I remembering the true definition of courage and doing them despite my fear?

Courage. Kindness. Friendship. Character.
These are the qualities that define us as human
beings, and propel us, on occasion, to greatness.
———R. J. PALACIO

Just the other day I heard a meditation teacher talk about how, after about five years, his meditation practice was adding to his life. Five years? I was hoping for five days. In this fast food nation, I know I tend to look for instant results, for something to be placed in front of me without any time or effort.

I am more and more compelled to live a "slow food" way of life, not just at mealtime but every day: remembering that each good thing I do in a day can build upon the day before it and lead me to a life worth living.

Let me dwell for a few minutes on this page. Let me be ready to read slowly, the next day taking just one page more, learning through ceaseless practice to instill in my life the qualities I value.

Can I find courage to slow down and practice
developing the qualities for which I long?

23

An apology includes real repair work: not just saying "I'm sorry." Often there will be nothing tangible to repair; hearts and relationships are broken more often than physical objects. In such cases, your efforts should focus on restoring the other person's dignity.

—MARTHA BECK

Growing up in an alcoholic home, I was sorry a lot. When I said, "I'm sorry," what I was seeking was some sort of release, a way to quickly make things better so I did not have to face consequences.

This kind of apology became a self-serving way to dismiss people in my adult life. Once I said I was sorry, the matter was closed. Why were other people still hurt or hanging onto their feelings about the situation?

In these cases, I was not honoring the other person's inherent worth and dignity, as my Unitarian Universalist faith calls me to do, and probably wasn't honoring my own, either. Acknowledging that we have worth and dignity means that we honor the range of emotions and hurts someone can experience. My apologies became a way to dismiss them.

By learning how to make amends, I have learned that an apology must also be followed by commitments and actions. It isn't just about words. And I've also learned that sometimes the amends aren't enough, and we have to just live with that. The focus must be on what the other person needs to feel their own sense of dignity and worth again.

What can I do to honor another's inherent worth and dignity today?

You can love them, forgive them, want good things for them . . . but still move on without them.

—MANDY HALE

It takes tremendous courage to let go of people, places, and things in our lives when they are detrimental to who we have become or who we wish to be. I now realize that I used to take this fact either too seriously or not seriously enough.

At first, I spent an inordinate amount of time trying to devise ways and explanations for how and why I could remain in close contact with the people, places, and things of my past life. I told myself I could continue to socialize with the people from my past life and be an example to inspire them to change. I told myself I could accept that we had different plans and goals but that I could still remain connected to them, because, in a phase attributed to early Unitarian Francis David, "We don't need to think alike to love alike."

Finally, I accepted that I had to let go of the old people, places, and things. But even then, I thought I could just step away and be done with them. I didn't realize for a while that I had to have the courage to grieve.

Am I allowing myself to grieve for the people, places, and things I had to leave?

25

*There is a strong element of faith in courage—
faith in the truth of who we are and where that
will lead us, faith in what we are doing and its
importance and value in the lives of others.*

—BARBARA BONNER

One of the symptoms of addiction is a tendency toward isolation. Even when I'm saying, "No, not me—I'm right in the middle of everything," if I look honestly, I'll see ways I have isolated myself from messages I didn't want to hear, things I didn't want to see. I separated myself from others by not being truly present even when I was with them in physical form.

I'm not going to be able to flip things right away, as if suddenly I'll see the burning bush and understand what has been wrong all along. But day by day, things will get better, so that when reviewing my behavior, I will see that there is a faith that journeys with me, accompanying me on a path to self-worth and service to others.

Courage is a long-haul skill. It moves slowly, stealthily, quietly. But it's worth the effort. It's a piece of my serenity.

———————

Where might I feel my faith in who I am today?

I find I am constantly being encouraged to pluck out some one aspect of myself and present this as the meaningful whole, eclipsing or denying the other parts of self.

—AUDRE LORDE

As I began the process of making my Ninth Step amends, I reached out to folks I felt I had harmed in the past to seek ways to right the wrongs. Along the way, a few folks had nothing but glowing things to say about me. Usually, we had a different recollection or interpretation of what had gone on. In this process where I had expected to do a lot of apologizing, their praise really didn't seem to fit the bill.

When I take a step back now to see what there was to learn from these situations, I wonder if the universe was showing me my whole self. While I wanted to focus on all of the wrong I had done, the universe wanted to hold me in balance, to allow me to see places where I was thinking I had done worse by others than I actually had. Each one of us is a whole person, neither inherently good nor inherently bad; we are a mix, holding the capacity to harm and to bless. Being shown who I am in my entirety was a gift of Step Nine.

Where do I believe things are worse than they actually are in my life?

If there was no fear, how could there be comfort? Or courage?

—VERONICA ROSSI

It takes courage to have faith, and it takes courage to hope. Faith is belief without evidence, or possibly belief despite evidence to the contrary. Hope is a belief in the possibility of a beneficent outcome despite a grim outlook. Faith and hope require courage, because with faith and hope there is the potential for the pain of failure. Courage is daring to maintain faith and hope despite past failures and despite the potential pain of failing yet again.

I had become acquainted with this principle in my athletic days. I knew that failure need not be final and that it is the courage to continue after failure that results in performing well. However, I had not realized that this is true not just in athletics but also in the battles of our lives.

We have all heard that courage does not mean being fearless. Courage is proceeding with faith and hope despite fear. This is the courage that is required for living well.

---

*Am I finding ways to accept my fear and
continue to nurture my hope and faith
despite past failures?*

Act as if what you do makes a difference. It does.
—WILLIAM JAMES

Have you thought back on how much your fourth-grade teacher made a difference in your life? Or a coach you had? Maybe they made a smaller difference, but have you thought about a time when a stranger held a door for you or another driver let you merge into traffic when you were having a rough day? Have you reflected on how something you appreciate could not have been there if someone hadn't made an effort?

You can be part of this equation—already are, actually. What you do is already making a difference, and when you begin to act from that knowledge, you make a greater difference than you did before.

It matters that people show up to our congregations on Sunday mornings, because their presence makes the community more vibrant and more appealing to new people. If you are a member of a faith community—or of any community—it matters how you treat people there, not only greeting friends but also welcoming someone new who might be apprehensive about coming in. Invite them to join you as you get coffee or find a seat. You are making a difference.

---

*How might I change my behavior to act as if
what I do makes a difference?*

29

Emotional intelligence is your ability to recognize and understand emotions in yourself and others, and your ability to use this awareness to manage your behavior and relationships.

—TRAVIS BRADBERRY

Behavioral scientists describe things called emotional intelligence, emotional competence, and emotional courage. Emotional courage is the courage to open ourselves to feeling the full spectrum of emotions, including the negative ones.

I now realize that I grew up thinking that emotions were of little or no value and that strong emotions required immediate action. Much of my youth was focused on managing and tolerating emotions. I now realize that at the root of my addictive behavior was the desire to manage, tolerate, or numb my feelings. I feared that if I allowed myself to feel fully, the pain would be unbearable.

With the use of mindfulness practices, I have come to know that I can slowly permit myself to feel emotions without permitting them to consume me. I can explore my emotions honestly, with the knowledge that they are not all of me. I can often examine them and let them pass, without any need to act immediately.

Am I making space for my emotions?

The moment we begin to fear the opinions of others and hesitate to tell the truth that is in us, and from motives of policy are silent when we should speak, the divine floods of light and life no longer flow into our souls.

—ELIZABETH CADY STANTON

When I was a kid, standing up for myself often meant risking my parent's rage. I learned to be quiet. To remain as well behaved and quiet as I possibly could. If I stayed this way, my theory went, I would never get yelled at—or perhaps my parent would even stop drinking entirely. Maybe it was because of my behavior that they drank in the first place.

When I became an adult, this learned behavior turned into never wanting to speak my mind because to do so felt risky. To speak up risked people being mad at me or disapproving of me or deciding to leave.

But, as I worked my program more, what I realized was that keeping all of this stuff inside only led to resentment. In recovery and through getting honest, I was able to see ways this behavior led me to have only shallow relationships and friendships. Over time, I learned to speak my mind in an honest way, recognizing that folks could disagree with me without raging at me. I was able to step into adult relationships more easily, without responding in old ways that did not honor my growth.

Where can I courageously speak my mind in relationship with others today?

October

Continued to take personal
inventory and when we were
wrong promptly admitted it.

1

The reward for living is the living itself.
—Charles Hartshorne

Folx in the throes of addiction find all kinds of reasons for using their substance. It's there for them when they're going through a hard time, kind of like a reward for having to endure difficulties. They say something like "I deserve a drink!" Or maybe it's shopping or some other behavior, rather than a substance, that they're addicted to.

In my time in recovery from addictive behavior, I have seen people go through all kinds of loss and trauma. They get through it by connecting to their Higher Power, through other friends in recovery, and by engaging in healthy community building and spiritual practice each day.

Unitarian Universalists do not believe in a punishing God. I do not believe in an omnipotent God but one who is with us in joy and in sorrow. The reward for living is the living itself.

———————

What kind of Higher Power do I connect to?
Will my Higher Power companion me
in the hard times?

Faith seeks understanding, and in doing so it turns to philosophy. Philosophical reason can be informed by faith; but only if the faith accepts correction at the hands of reason and experience can it be also an informed, a dependable, faith.

—Rev. James Luther Adams

When I first entered recovery, I mistook hard work for discipline, and the harder I worked to fix myself, the worse things became. With every false start and potential "fall off the wagon," my self-esteem sank lower. I was sure that I was a bad mother, an inconsiderate spouse, and a weak person.

With my sponsor's support, I put down the drink and picked up recovery's spiritual toolkit. With my newfound approaches to life—including regular meeting attendance, open sharing with trusted friends, and living with honesty, openness, and willingness—I began to recover. I followed my sponsor's suggestions and went to ninety meetings in ninety days. I prayed each morning and spent time journaling. I worked the Steps as if my life depended on it, because it did, even though it didn't look that way from the outside.

Today I live an imperfect but disciplined life, and I love it. I go to meetings, work a Tenth Step on fears and resentments as they crop up, and spend time in prayer, meditation, and journaling every morning. These disciplines free me to be the person I am called to be.

What disciplines has recovery taught me? How is my life easier and more fulfilling when I do them?

*As we move through life
finding ourselves,
always newly wise and newly foolish,
we ask that our mistakes be small
and not hurtful.*

—Rev. Orlanda Brugnola

This life is a journey of continual growth in mind, body, and spirit. The learning never stops, no matter how much wisdom we think we possess. We are always newly wise and newly foolish.

The discipline of regularly checking in with ourselves about times when we have been selfish, dishonest, self-seeking, or afraid helps us grow. Our awareness shifts, and we find ourselves looking for where we have fallen short, not out of shame or self-hate but rather out of curiosity and with our hearts turned toward righting the things we have said or done that have caused harm. We seek to right the mistakes rather than to have them remain hanging over our heads.

To recover is to continue on a path of consistent spiritual growth and maturity. To recover is to seek spaces where we can bring the divine in, rather than holding on to our shortcomings as some sort of shameful secret. To recover is to be both wise about our actions and in "beginner's mind" on a regular basis. May we hold both wisdom and curiosity tenderly and continue to learn and grow.

Where am I noticing my own spiritual growth?

They flatly declare that since they have come to
believe in a Power greater than themselves . . .
there has been a revolutionary change in their way
of living and thinking.

—ALCOHOLICS ANONYMOUS, "THE BIG BOOK"

Belief in a Higher Power, however we understand that Higher Power, is foundational to recovery. You would think that this would be familiar to those of us who are Unitarian Universalists. Our tradition draws on the world's religions, humanist teachings, and direct personal experience to help us in our journey of spiritual development. We believe that there is no one pathway to truth and that every person has the right to a personal understanding of truth. You might think, therefore, that AA's encouragement to come to our own understanding of what a Higher Power is would be familiar and easy.

Yet I had layers of misconceptions, fears, and prejudices within me to discover and discard. Slowly but surely, I have come to an understanding of a Higher Power that works for me. Equally important, I have come to know, or experience, that Higher Power, not just think about it.

I find myself better able to sit in the program, and in my church, with people who are on their own spiritual journeys. I can offer assurance from personal experience that it is a journey of discovery that works. Its rewards are far greater than any drink or substance has ever given me.

Can I give myself permission to trust the timing
of my spiritual growth and development?

When I first got sober in 1985 . . . I was not big on the idea of calling strangers with my problems. But I knew that I was a wreck, that those people at the meetings were not wrecks, and that I wanted to be a former wreck and get what they had. And lo and behold, when I called them, suddenly they weren't strangers anymore.

—JUDITH H.

In early recovery, making a phone call was one of the most difficult things for me. I had an alcoholic mother who used to spend hours on the telephone every night in a drunken stupor. I defended myself in childhood by hiding, and I was shy and uncomfortable around people.

Getting to my first AA meeting was hard. Asking someone to be my sponsor was harder. Calling three recovered people every day, on the advice of my sponsor, was hardest of all. Yet my desire to recover was stronger than my resistance. My sponsor told me that it was the surest defense if I found myself wanting to drink. By calling people every day, I would have a network of friends I could talk to, and making calls would grow easier.

Today I pick up the phone without a thought. It is a joy to talk with my friends about recovery and about life. Our phone calls always lift me up, even when I hadn't realized I was down.

———————

How has picking up the telephone or not picking up the telephone affected my recovery? Who am I going to call today?

*We've become so addicted to instant gratification
that we're blind to the impact it has on our lives.*

—FRANK SONNENBERG

The spiritual component in Twelve-Step recovery is based on "a power greater than ourselves." It works when no amount of willpower has been able to remove the addictive craving.

But it doesn't mean that a simple program does not involve some hard work. It could be that willpower is something marshaled alone and that the discipline needed in successful recovery work comes through the support of that Higher Power that so often shows itself in other people.

One suggestion for working on discipline is to get a plant and see if you can keep it alive. It requires discipline to pay attention to how often it needs watering, to remember to care about it day after day. Can you do that? Now you might be able to be counted on to do something more important. Not that a plant isn't important.

How might I demonstrate discipline today?

I want to be with people who give of themselves, who share their hearts and minds and gifts. I want to be with people who know that human community is often warm and generous, sometimes challenging and almost always a grand adventure.

—REV. DANA E. WORSNOP

It is amazing how different our life experiences can be and yet how similar some issues that underlie our struggles can be. In my commitment to the Tenth Step, I often find myself talking to people in my recovery program about fears or resentments we both hold. We can be talking about entirely different people in our lives. And yet we are both struggling with control, or with living with other people's disapproval, or even with what happens when things do not go according to our plans and designs.

I love that moment of recognition because it helps me to honestly face the deeper parts of myself that are in need of healing, in a way that assures me I am not alone. It doesn't necessarily soften the impact of the harms we might have caused in the lives of our spouses or our roommates. Instead, it helps to put our behavior in perspective and gives us mutual strength to approach our loved ones and make amends.

I no longer need to feel separate and apart in my struggles, to feel that other people are strangers. Instead, I can feel connected to people through our common human struggles and how we directly address them.

———

How can I connect with others around our shared struggles?

We delight in the beauty of the butterfly,
but rarely admit the changes it has gone through to
*   achieve that beauty.*

—MAYA ANGELOU

I thought that recovery was all about putting down my substance of choice, but I soon realized it was about much more.

The emotional pain that food had numbed for so many years surfaced soon after I stopped eating sugar. To deal with this pain, I turned first to well-worn defense mechanisms, including lashing out and blaming others. It was clear these also needed to transform. I needed to replace people-pleasing with self-care. Practicing self-care showed me I needed to work less and rest more. So many things needed to change that these changes couldn't, and didn't, happen all at once or overnight.

I let go of behaviors and attitudes that had plagued me. New things took their place. I took up hobbies and interests I had long forgotten. I continued doing the things that were fostering critical changes. I attended meetings, called my sponsor, and did daily inventories. I kept doing them until I no longer had to do them. And then I did them because I wanted to.

Now I have tools that can help shift my mood. Inventories are some of the most powerful tools. I enter each day more or less free of the build-up of repressed emotions.

———————

When is the last time that I took a personal inventory?

*There is too much hardship in this world to not
    find joy, every day
There is too much injustice in this world to not
    right the balance, every day
There is too much pain in this world to not heal,
    every day*

—Rev. Darcy Roake

One year, our church's stewardship theme was "Let's Show Up!" It felt so fitting for this group of people who had been consistently showing up all over our community for justice causes, for moments of sorrow and celebration, and for one another.

So much of what we do in recovery is continually showing up. Showing up to meetings. Showing up when someone gives us a call or when we are a part of a sponsor–sponsee relationship. Showing up to listen to someone who is new and struggling, as well as to folks who are in longtime recovery and still struggle. One of my recovery teachers continually repeats, "This is not a program for folks who need it. It's a program for folks who work it."

And so recovery becomes an everyday process. It becomes an everyday part of our lives, whether we are showing up in our relationships in recovery rooms or we are showing up for our families, our workplaces, our communities. Let's show up!

---

*Where can I show up for someone
other than myself today?*

There is so much to forgive in this world.
Those who have been hurt often know that best.
—REV. JOHN BUEHRENS

After completing my first Fourth Step inventory, I realized that I had given a tremendous amount of power to other people. My fear of others' not liking me masked a deep-seated fear of abandonment. I would lose myself by giving in to the opinions of others, saying "yes" when I wanted to say "no." It was often difficult for me to make simple decisions, like what movie to watch or what to eat for dinner, without agonizing over what those in my family wanted.

Working my program brought me face to face with how fear ran my life. The origins of my fear became clear as I recovered. A lot of it stemmed from being raised in an alcoholic home. If I was to live free from fear, I needed to forgive those who hurt me and forgive myself for hurting others.

I learned that prayer works: it changed me. I prayed to forgive the people who hurt me, and I asked to be shown compassion. I made amends to the people I had hurt.

Over the years my relationships transformed, and they are still transforming. Fear plays a smaller role in my life, and love has slowly and surely become the center of my existence.

Am I willing to pray for the willingness to
forgive myself and others?

With integrity, you have nothing to fear,
since you have nothing to hide. With integrity,
you will do the right thing, so you will have
no guilt.

—ZIG ZIGLER

One of the slogans in my program is "just do the next right thing." It's a great guide to follow when I just don't know what to do, or when I'm obsessed with something to the point of being overwhelmed by it.

Sometimes discipline can feel like a need to control, but it's actually so often just about making my bed, brushing my teeth, making that phone call, doing the next right thing.

I can get overwhelmed with work, or even more with things that I feel I'm not very good at, like preparing my taxes. Doing the next right thing is like taking one bite at a time. I don't need to eat the whole elephant today.

What is the next right thing?
Would making a list help?

We make the choice to stay stuck together even when we don't even want to be in the same room. But we always come back to the table, because we choose to be together. Through thick and thin, we have chosen love.

—EMMA MERCHANT

If you had told me that I would spend a good portion of my days apologizing and taking action to be in better relationship with my spouse and chosen family, I might have not even started this recovery journey.

But this is the work, because these are the folks I often hurt the most. These are the folks who see me when I am at my messiest. These are the people whose toes I step on, whose hurts I hurdle past, whose inherent worth and dignity it is sometimes hard for me to see.

To remain dedicated to spiritual growth, to remain dedicated to lifelong learning, I must learn some lessons by repetition. And I wish I did not have to learn them at the expense of others. What I know is that we are often going through our days causing harm without even knowing it— and with no way to acknowledge or repair it. What I know is that those who love me, who are willing to hear me out and willing to hold me to the commitments I make, these are the folks I want to continue to grow alongside.

Who in my life continually comes back to the table with me? Where can I show them some appreciation?

13

Spirit of Love, help us never to forget: we are your voice, hands, eyes, and ears and heart upon this one precious Earth. Help us to live in peace together and serve one another and to see the holy light in everyone, even when those holy lights are especially hard to see.

—REV. DANIEL GREGOIRE

To see those we despise in a holy light is such hard spiritual work. It asks us to set aside all that we think we know about another person, to keep an open mind and heart as we interact with them or listen to them. This is one of the deepest challenges to my Universalist theology. Even *that* person is held by universal love? Are you sure?

My theology and our shared recovery programs remind me, and all of us, that that person has their own lesson to learn. We are not qualified to stand in judgment over anyone else. Each one of us is flawed. People have held similar resentments toward us for our own behavior.

Today we seek ways to process our resentments, our fears, and the ways we have harmed others through spiritual practice and continually making amends where they are needed. It is a difficult task to make amends to those we think are wrong or those we dislike. We focus on our actions and our words and strive to treat others with the love and kindness they deserve.

Whose holy lights are hardest for me to see?
Where can I bring them into my spiritual practice?

"Where's your church?"
"We're standing in it."
"But this is a bookstore and it's a Friday."
　　　　　—REV. FORREST CHURCH

I wonder if people know how spectacular their church basements are, how many lives are saved by coming there day after day, how many truths get spoken, and how many arms are outstretched in understanding.

Do people who come to church on Sundays realize that there is a sacred text, called the "big book," stored in plastic bins in closets all around them? How reading and then doing what this text describes moves people from addiction to wholeness to helping?

Has anyone shared the good news with them that their church is saving lives by opening its doors, basements, and fellowship halls?

Would they consider measuring their church's vitality not only by the number of people in attendance each Sunday morning but also by the number of recovery meetings that happen in the building each week?

We would tell them if we could, but anonymity is the spiritual foundation of all our traditions, and we operate by attraction rather than promotion.

For now, I will keep coming back into these holy spaces, the basements and fellowship halls.

———————

*Do I have a home group? Is going to meetings
a part of my plan of recovery?*

We come to gather strength from each other.
We come to give strength to each other.
We come to ask for strength from the Spirit of
All That Is and Is Not.

—Rev. Marta I. Valentín

The solidarity and strength in our rooms are palpable. We open our hearts and share from deep inside. I have heard people who were taller than professional basketball players talk about being afraid and people much smaller in stature describe rage inside of them so big that it could kill. "Our secrets kill," we are taught, and so we talk.

The kindness and generosity in the rooms of recovery are real and unfettered. It doesn't matter who people are outside of the rooms. When we are together, we are one—one sober person sharing experience, strength, and hope with another; one person trying again. And we are many people waiting to welcome each person back.

We identify with one another because we know that our recovery depends on it. We do not discuss politics, religion, and other outside issues because they divert us from our reason for being together. Each time we leave a meeting, we bring more of these practices into the rest of our lives.

What is one thing that we do in the rooms of AA
that I can bring into my interactions outside
of our meetings today?

Three things I pray
To see thee more clearly
Love thee more dearly
Follow thee more nearly
Day by day

—"DAY BY DAY," FROM *GODSPELL*

I was a Unitarian Universalist teen when my high school choir did a review of *Godspell*. It was a few years after the movie had come out, adapted from the play; both were inspired by parables from the Gospel of Matthew and lyrics taken from hymns.

I was a musical theater junkie, and my friends and I would gather in someone's living room to sit and sing all the songs from the show. I loved it.

Yet I was a UU, and an agnostic humanist one at that, so my love for the music led me to a lot of translating. I had to translate the language of the songs into concepts that didn't conflict with my own beliefs.

Now, as an older adult, I can still call upon the translation skills I learned as a teen and remember the beauty of the lyrics I repeated so long ago. Day by day I call upon the Spirit of Life to help me see things more clearly, love more dearly, and follow the Ultimate more nearly. Day by day.

———

Can I be inspired day by day?

Sometimes I am adrift in my faith, all at sea.
I must remind myself that not only can I swim,
But I can read the sun and the moon.
I know the smell of the storm on the horizon.

—REV. ADAM LAWRENCE DYER

If I was going to stay sober, feeling powerless had to change. The paradox of needing to admit my powerlessness over addictive substances and to also stop living as a victim was real. Sometimes I stay in fear and resentment longer than I need to because it feels safer that way. Working the Steps repeatedly and experiencing the freedom that inevitably follows lead me to trust and rely on them.

Today when resentment is brewing in me or a fear is pestering me, I pick up my pen and write as quickly as possible. Even taking five minutes to write or talk with someone in recovery can be transformative.

No longer do I have to live feeling at the mercy of people around me. When I feel resentments and fears as a sober person today, I see them as barometers telling me to step back and right myself. They are sure signs that something is amiss within me. Rather than allowing them to lead me back to a drink, I thank them for showing up, and I turn to our tools to release them.

What happens in my mind or body when I
experience a resentment or fear?

We are one,
A diverse group
Of proudly kindred spirits
Here, not by coincidence—
But because we choose to journey—together.

—REV. HOPE JOHNSON

Learning to identify with people and not compare myself to them is a skill that keeps me sober. Approaching meetings with this attitude allows me to listen to how people feel and not to how much they did or didn't drink. I realize that I am not unique in my feelings. Other people feel just like me. Together we learn to ask if this way of thinking is true and helpful or if it needs to change. We learn from one another and try living the way that people we admire in the rooms are living.

"Does it need to be said? Does it need to be said now? Does it need to be said by me?" The practice of asking these questions has guided me in developing self-restraint.

We are brought together as addicts by our common problems. We thrive together as people in recovery. We become people of integrity and grace. We see the good in others and in ourselves. We choose to see how we are alike and focus on our common humanity.

We are stronger because of each other.

How can I identify with someone new today?

On the other hand—and strange as this may seem to those who do not understand—once a psychic change has occurred, the very same person who seemed doomed, who had so many problems he despaired of ever solving them, suddenly finds himself easily able to control his desire for alcohol, the only effort necessary being that required to follow a few simple rules.

—ALCOHOLICS ANONYMOUS,
"THE BIG BOOK"

Discipline often brings a gift. I often tend to think of the word in hard terms, that *discipline* means something painful or harsh.

It's good to remember that discipline often is only hard at the outset, and then it brings with it a flow, an ease of movement.

In the case of the obsession of addiction, once a "psychic change" has taken place, the effort needed is simply to stick with the practice. I believe I've found a spiritual gift.

———————

How am I looking at the word "discipline"?

Steadfastness is a lovely, old-fashioned word that we don't hear much about these days. . . . Steadfast people . . . stand clear in their beliefs, grounded in their cause, faithful to the end. . . . And once we find each other, we need to support and encourage our steadfast behaviors.

—Margaret Wheatley

Years ago, I developed a practice of texting my friend in recovery every morning to share our thoughts on the meditation of the day. It keeps us connected and has strengthened our friendship, even when one of us moved to another state. It challenges us to consider the words we are reading and reduces the chance of their becoming rote.

We try to share specific examples of how the reading applies to our lives, but the practice is helpful even when we share a more general response to what we have read. Our texts are often the springboard into journaling, which is the next thing that I do each morning.

From there I move to centering prayer, which further develops my steadfastness and centeredness. I begin each day renewed and ready to enter into the stream of life.

Done without fail over time, these morning practices have become an important part of my recovery and provide an anchor in the fullness of life. Through these practices, I see the steadfast gifts of recovery.

What helps me to develop the quality of steadfastness?

21

The greatest learning has come from feeling my fears, my losses, my dreams, and even my quest to "find me," transformed through the experience of finding and feeling we.

—REV. DAVID RUFFIN

For a time, I believed the Tenth Step was all about finding my faults and pointing them out. It was something I often did in isolation, seeing where I fell short of my aspiration to treat others kindly or be in right relationship with my spouse.

We are asked to reach out to someone who is also in recovery to share our fears, our resentments, and the ways we have caused harm. In the process we are listened to, and reflection is offered back. It is also a time when we turn from sharing to helping others, to being of service in our homes and in our communities. This is not a part of the program that we do alone. In fact, no part of the program is supposed to be done in isolation.

What I love about this Step now are the moments when I am listening or sharing and I hear a common story. Moments when I know I can relate to the person sharing because I have done the same thing. And moments when another can relate to me because they have said the same thing to someone else. What a gift to know we are not alone in our everyday struggles toward spiritual growth and wholeness.

When has there been a moment of hearing my truth in the story of another?

We can either make ourselves miserable or we make ourselves strong. The amount of work is the same.

—GEORGE MUMFORD

I used to make a mess of all kinds of things. My file cabinets, my kitchen sink, my relationships with people.

I never thought that stopping drinking would result in a clean house and healthier relationships. And the primary purpose of my recovery group is to help people stay sober and help others to achieve sobriety. But there are great gifts that come with sobriety that I could have never imagined.

I am more careful with my finances, with my work, with the way I care about my family members.

I feel a great sense of joy after this "cleanup." Instead of focusing on drinking, I can focus on living a good life.

———————

Do I want to be miserable or strong?

23

I've been trying to cultivate appreciation, to see the merits of what's in front of me instead of the flaws, even if they're not my taste. I still catch myself in critique mode—it's hard to unlearn—but overall, I'm a happier person with indiscriminate tastes.

—KAT LIU

To be in a mode of appreciation and gratitude takes attention. It is not something that always comes naturally, especially in a culture that pits certain attributes against one another. Strong versus weak. Pretty versus ugly. Winners versus losers.

In addiction, we often see life in extremes—one versus the other. It is hard to get to a both/and place because we have to acknowledge the middle ground. It's not just that that person was rude to me but that they are also hurting and experiencing more than I can see. It's not just that the drugs or the drinks make me feel good but also that I need better coping mechanisms to help me deal with a host of experiences.

To live outside of these false binaries and extremes takes dedication and constant attention. It is not about one versus the other. It is about appreciating what is in the here and now. Living life free from this competition mode of one over the other. Living a life of appreciation.

---

*Where can I bring my attention
and appreciation today?*

Read some good, heavy, serious books just for discipline: Take yourself in hand and master yourself.

—W. E. B. Du Bois

I love the idea of spiritual practice as a form of discipline. It may be that we are already reading "heavy" books but haven't thought of them as a way to "master" ourselves.

As someone recovering from addiction, I need a little more self-compassion, yet not so much that I wallow in self-pity.

So I need the reminders. To take myself in hand, and keep up with the daily practice. Reading some spiritual inspiration, connecting with others, sitting in meditation, attending a meeting are all things that move me toward mastery, or as I like to call it, spiritual maturity.

What can I do today to continue a compassionate discipline?

25

All successful life is / Adaptable, / Opportunistic, / Tenacious, / Interconnected, and / Fecund. / Understand this. / Use it. / Shape God.

—OCTAVIA BUTLER

I regularly come into contact with new social justice projects that aim to do good work and activate more members of my Unitarian Universalist faith. Discovering these projects is a joy, and learning what people are doing to have hope in our world helps me be more creative.

I'm also being challenged by adrienne maree brown's concept of "emergent strategy," where we aim to pay attention to complex systems and patterns arising out of relatively simple interactions. It feels tough to think of new ways of doing things in this time of accelerating climate change, racial injustice, and daily national strife. But it also feels hopeful. We can notice small actions and connections and see how they create complex systems.

As someone who lives with addiction, I have often found it hard to live life on life's terms. I want to control what is happening around me and have others follow my script. This happens both in small interactions as well as on a larger scale in the movements for justice I am a part of. Leaning into our interconnectedness helps me to see that there is something larger at work than my own plans and designs.

How might I value small-scale growth and change? Where might I find a place to learn, and with whom might I learn?

True belonging doesn't require us to change who we are. It requires us to be who we are.
—BRENÉ BROWN

Who was I? When I was in active addiction, it was hard to say. I could be whatever the world required of me, especially if it meant I would be able to keep using. I had friends whose values were fundamentally irreconcilable with mine, but we were in relationship at the time because we used together.

This recovery process, and especially Step Ten, has allowed me to learn more about who I am. Regularly looking at my part in fears, harms, and resentments can provide a pretty powerful mirror. Sharing with others has helped me to reflect on patterns of being and areas of growth.

I no longer feel as if I need to sacrifice who I am in order to find friends or get what I need. Instead, recovery has helped me to be more honest about myself. I can now lead with who I am and find places where I truly belong.

Where do I authentically belong?

I had to learn, really, how to rein in my energies and discipline myself. And I found it very, very, useful. I rebelled against it at first, but it's a good thing to have.

—Patti Smith

It's not surprising that I don't like the idea of discipline. I'm a Unitarian Universalist, after all. I pride myself in liking the questions, in being a little outside the box, in being an individual. I tend to be suspicious of things that everybody else does. Like Twelve-Step programs.

But what I have found is that discipline can also allow for creativity. By first taking care of what I need to do, I gain more space to do what I want.

My experience has demonstrated that Twelve-Step wisdom has been used by many kinds of people, over many years, and my willingness to stick with it has led to great success.

Is my pushing back against the idea of a program keeping me from success?

Return again, return again
Return to the land of your soul.
　　—RABBI SCHLOMO CARLEBACH

Each week, like clockwork, I return to the same fear. It doesn't quite matter what it is, but the feeling and the thought process are familiar. Perhaps you too have fears that keep coming up in your life over and over again. The same old story you are telling yourself about what will happen.

What's wild about this fear is that it never comes true, even though I keep returning to it.

Through the Tenth Step process of bringing this fear to a fellow and to my Higher Power, I constantly receive a message saying, "Trust." Trust that all will work out. Trust that this fear will not materialize. Trust that all is as it needs to be. Trust that even if this fear does materialize, I will continue to be held by something larger and will likely survive. This fear, whether mine or yours, is not life-threatening. Trust in this process. Trust in your fellow human beings. In the face of a recurring fear, trust.

————————

Where can I embrace trust in the face of fear?

29

Now, discipline always seems painful rather than pleasant at the time, but later it yields the peaceful fruit of righteousness to those who have been trained by it.

—HEBREWS 12:11

Admiral William R. McRaven said to the graduating class at the University of Texas, "If you make your bed every morning you will have accomplished the first task of the day. It will give you a small sense of pride, and it will encourage you to do another task and another and another. By the end of the day, that one task completed will have turned into many tasks completed. Making your bed will also reinforce the fact that little things in life matter. If you can't do the little things right, you will never do the big things right."

This advice follows the same principle as recovery work. Doing the next right thing moves me to make good habits. And good habits make for a virtuous life. If I start with making my bed in the morning, my chances improve for the health of the rest of the day.

Can I feel a small sense of "right-sized" pride by doing the next right thing?

Of course, the truth is that slow progress is not a failure. Slow progress is still better than nothing.
—Jami Gold

For years in my program, I kept relapsing and coming right back, only to go into relapse again six months later. I was in a cycle that I couldn't seem to get out of.

When I finally got sober for good (one day at a time), what I recognized was that my substance was still an option for me until it wasn't any longer. It was still an option for me until I was willing to see how much that substance had devastated my life and just how hopeless and powerless it had left me.

What I have learned from the stories of others, and from my own story, is that some of us are just slow learners. Some of us need to keep coming back again and again because there is something we have missed. Something we still need to learn. It takes discipline to keep coming back to the table over and over again. And the sober life I live now is so much better than where I've been before. The slow progress really got me to a life beyond my imagining.

———————

Where can I embrace and accept my slow progress?

*Listen widely to remove your doubts
and be careful when speaking about
the rest and your mistakes will be few.*

—Confucius

So much of recovery has been learning to listen. Listening to the experiences of others. Listening to someone who is new to recovery and struggling. Listening to my own heart when the old behaviors come creeping back with a vengeance.

As I began regularly attending to the Tenth Step of recovery and taking daily inventory, there were times when folks shared feedback I would rather not have heard. There were times when they saw character defects in play that I had missed or even amends I owed that I had not noticed. At first, I was dismissive, but I eventually learned that these folks were only attempting to be helpful to me.

Through listening to these fellows and taking action where I could, I have grown. I can better see where my character defects are at play. I have become more ready to make regular amends. It doesn't all happen perfectly, but there are lessons here I never would have learned if I had not been willing to listen.

———————

Where can I be quick to listen today?

November

Sought through prayer and
meditation to improve our
conscious contact with God, as we
understood God, praying only for
knowledge of God's will for us and
the power to carry that out.

NOVEMBER

1

Let us open our hearts, still our minds and enter a time of prayer.

Let us call forth and hold in our hearts the stories of all who have come before us, the memories of those who are with us today, and the hope for tomorrow and for all of those who will come after us.

—Rev. Viola Abbitt

Let us make time for some quiet meditation in this day. Step Eleven reads, "Sought through prayer and meditation to increase our conscious contact with God as we understood God, praying only for knowledge of God's will and the power to carry that out." Today, we pause to listen, to embrace silence, and to seek the will of a Higher Power of our understanding. Set aside the hecticness of your to-do list; put out of your mind and heart your plans for the days and weeks ahead. Take some time today to just sit in quiet, to embrace the stillness.

Hymn 352 in the Unitarian Universalist songbook *Singing the Living Tradition* invites us to sing "Find a stillness, hold a stillness, let the stillness carry me." As you listen to the stillness today, pay attention to where you are being carried. Surrender to the journey you are being called to.

However silence and meditation look to you, make intentional time today to embrace them. May your spirit be filled by the time.

Can I take five or ten minutes today to sit in silence and just listen? What do I hear?

"When I was a boy and I would see scary things in the news, my mother would say to me, "Look for the helpers. You will always find people who are helping."
—FRED ROGERS

Last summer a massive wildfire hit my community hard. I listened closely to the experts saying that we should expect it to continue burning for a long while. They also told us that we had over five hundred firefighters and many teams working together to do their best to keep structures and people safe.

It was a scary time. I worried about my friends and family, about their businesses and homes. I took strength in my sobriety, which allows me to feel gratitude for firefighters and awe in the power of fire.

We have seen so many disasters, both natural and human-made. But every time, people work together to get through them, sending aid from near and far. Today I can look to be a helper to find ways to deepen our community connections.

What does my neighbor need that I may be able to give?

3

We receive fragments of holiness, glimpses of eternity, brief moments of insight. Let us gather them up for the precious gifts that they are, and, renewed by their grace, move boldly into the unknown.

—REV. SARAH YORK

In my recovery, sometimes I am not patient. I want to leap. I want to soar. I want to fly. I want to run that whole long victory lap. But this is not that time. This is not that moment. This is the moment to be grateful that I can hop, that I can flap a little on the ground. This is the time to be glad for precious determination and for the ability to walk slowly and steadily, feeling the good ground beneath my planted feet. The gratitude is enough. The healing will come, breath by breath, moment by moment.

I am grateful today for the opportunity to heal, for the opportunity to be present. I am grateful for the presence of more peace and more possibility. I am grateful for continuing resolve and for the chance to rest in gratitude, to heal in wholeness, to bask in awareness. Welcome, gratitude and awareness! I am grateful for the small gains and the small movements forward.

Today, how might I be grateful for the small movements forward toward healing, and for the precious hints that I am moving back toward the wholeness which is my birthright?

I give thanks
for all it takes
to be a healing presence,
and also how simple it is.

 —SAMANTHA GUPTA

Although I was born and raised Unitarian Universalist, my family did not embrace any form of spiritual practice at home. When I encountered it in church, it felt like a foreign concept to me. We would often hold space there to pray or to meditate, but even in church it wasn't part of our everyday routine.

Recovery has been huge in helping me to embrace a spiritual practice. Whether it is nightly gratitude lists or daily meditation, I am slowly learning that spiritual practice is a part of caring for myself and replenishing my energy. Even just the routine of going to meetings, similar to how I attended worship services, has been a healing touchstone of each week. I look forward to seeing the folks I care about. I look forward to the listening and the sharing.

I may not have been raised with spiritual practice as a part of my days, but now it's hard to imagine life without it. I feel more calm, less anxious, and more energized throughout each day. Of course, I still have problems. Now I just find better ways to deal with them.

What is a spiritual practice I feel drawn to?
What is drawing me there?

Direct experience of that transcending mystery and wonder, affirmed in all cultures, which moves us to a renewal of the spirit and an openness to the forces which create and uphold life.

—First Source of
Unitarian Universalism

The place where I live offers me direct and easy access to the natural world. I can walk safe paved or dirt trails just outside my door. I have easy access to the landscapes my Unitarian ancestor Ralph Waldo Emerson said we often use as the "emblems of our thoughts."

It hasn't always been this way for me, and it isn't now for many people, especially those on the margins. In some circumstances and places, we may not have such access and may need to look at other things or within ourselves, by using practices such as daily meditation, sitting in church, visiting an art museum, studying in the quietest part of the library, or even looking into the face of a stranger.

Spiritual practices can vary greatly. You might play your guitar every morning or swim laps while repeating prayers. Whatever we choose to do, whatever we are able to do, the purpose is spiritual development, quieting the mind, becoming renewed.

How have I been able to find transcending mystery and wonder in my spiritual practice?

There are only two ways to live your life.
One is as though nothing is a miracle.
The other is as though everything is a miracle.

—ATTRIBUTED TO ALBERT EINSTEIN

Sometimes, no matter what we plan, something else happens. And there it is and I face that choice: to close my mind or open my heart. And here it is: the blaze of color on an autumn day, the new vistas revealed by the falling of leaves. The things I never thought to know. The perspectives gained unnoticed.

As someone who prizes control, I have to choose to open my heart to the uninvited, to the unexpected. I have to convince myself to invite it in wholeheartedly. And yet when I do, I am always glad and grateful. The unplanned gifts are often the greatest.

Sense possibility, I tell myself—for it awaits beyond what can be known. Keep your heart as a welcome for the shy truth that seeks a home, I cajole. That way I can know joy when it arises down deep like a belly laugh in my soul. I can greet the unexpected like the friend I never knew I needed and yet who brings nourishment like a casserole dish for my soul. Through this practice, I can appreciate the new path that offers confusion and eventual resolution. I try, in this way, to welcome the unexpected.

―――――――

How can the delight of the unexpected allow me to
surrender to the larger will of the world, to give up
the need to always be in charge?

Let every moment be a prayer.
With every sip of tea,
let your lips move in thanksgiving.
—ELENA WESTBROOK

Breathe in deep. Release the air and empty your lungs. Repeat. Repeat. Repeat.

Spiritual practices aren't just about the intentional times we make at the beginning or the end of the day. They are also in the moments when our anxieties are high, when it feels like too much is going on, when our hearts are full and we just need a moment to pause.

Breathe in deep. Release the air and empty your lungs. Repeat. Repeat. Repeat.

Sometimes, I am in a meeting—a room full of people—and I just need a moment. Deep breaths are a spiritual practice I can engage in at any time. No one can tell I'm breathing deeply. But I can feel my shoulders relax, my body soften, and my mind grow less tense.

Throughout your day, when you are stressed or feeling tense or even resentful of those around you, may you find the strength to pause and breathe.

How do I know when I need to take a pause
and just breathe?

Heaps of black cherries
glittering with drops of rain
in the evening sun.

  —RICHARD WRIGHT

I love the work of food activist Bryant Terry. In his artfully illustrated cookbooks he includes sources of his inspiration, which include music, poetry, and people. In this month of connecting myself to a deeper relationship with my Higher Power, I find authentic nourishment through reading about cooking and about creating sustainable communities and in the act of creating healthy meals.

In this month especially, I remember my own mother's cooking and recall with deep appreciation one particularly delicious peach pie she made with an almond and coco-nut crust.

Food, and preparing it for others, are spiritual gifts we can give. They are ways of expressing love and gratitude.

———————

What gift can I give to another by preparing
or sharing food?

9

At times, our own light goes out and is rekindled by a spark from another person. Each of us has cause to think with deep gratitude of those who have lighted the flame within us.

—ALBERT SCHWEITZER

In a particularly hard time of my life, I would practice something I once heard in a meeting, which was to lie very still and to make a list of everything for which I was grateful. Sometimes I also do this with people—if I start to make a list of everyone who has added some good to my life, I find myself producing a very long list! Some people have helped me in big ways, and others have aided me in small ones. Whether small or large, when I am still and take an accounting, I can be overwhelmed by the wonder of it all.

Being touched by addiction and all the worries that it engenders can make it easy to focus on the negative and to be mired in all my worries and cares. I can also get caught in thinking only of those who have harmed me, intentionally or unintentionally. Just the simple act of listing all the people who have helped is liberating and empowering—a lens through which I can see the world as abundant.

This practice of counting my blessings is so satisfying that sometimes I do it just as I am falling asleep. The list is like an extra blanket, warming me and wrapping me in comfort throughout the night.

Who are the people who have helped me along the way? For whom am I especially grateful today?

When we experience the full presence of each other,
Because of our shared humanity,
Because of our differences,
That is where holy gratitude begins.

—REV. ANDRÉE MOL

Gratitude engaged in as a spiritual practice has a way of reorienting our brains. One sponsor I used to work with would ask me at the end of our calls, after I had spent so much time talking about my problems, "What are you grateful for in this situation?" I found myself feeling grateful for the things that had been annoying me just a moment ago, for the lessons I was learning, for moments when I was aware there was a larger design in play than what I saw as my own needs.

The more I embrace gratitude, the less I get bent out of shape about in my life. The less time I spend thinking people should do one thing or another. The less I argue with my spouse or my co-workers.

Gratitude has brought me to a place of really cherishing the gifts that are all around, not the least of which is the life I have been given, which I have reclaimed through my spiritual recovery.

―――――――――

What am I grateful for in this very moment?

"Age" is the acceptance of a term of years.
But maturity is the glory of years.

—MARTHA GRAHAM

Years ago, at a central office for Twelve-Step meetings, I picked up a little folded wallet card listing sixteen elements of what it called "emotional maturity." It indicated that the list was taken from a text titled *Moral and Spiritual Values in Education,* used by the Los Angeles City Schools. The language was old-fashioned and the publication was decades old, but the qualities listed seemed to be things I was still lacking, despite my graduate-level education. Two of the sixteen elements still strike me: "this person meets emergencies with poise," and "their feelings are not easily hurt."

Years later, looking again at this values list, I know I am much better able to meet emergencies without yelling or coming undone, but I still start out with a shock. My feelings are no longer easily hurt, but I do often still stew about something that's been said to me.

A slogan I hear repeatedly says, "Progress, not perfection." I am glad that I have so many tools available to aid me in moving toward emotional and spiritual maturity. I'm going to keep on.

How was my maturity yesterday?
Might I look for progress today?

*We wish for the abundance of this world
to be shared, for fear to become love, for the
lonely to feel welcomed, and for the suffering
to know rest and joy.*

—Rev. Naomi King

A Unitarian Universalist hymn begins, "For all that is our life, we sing our thanks and praise." I have days when offering thanks and praise can seem like a huge challenge, and yet just that line, sung or recited again and again, can be a mantra that calls me into my best self, into the mindfulness that can tame the anxious chatter in my head.

If, each time I sing or say those lines, I think of one thing for which I am grateful—and if I repeat it enough times—I can sometimes feel gratitude settling around me like a companionable presence. My life, when seen as worthy of thanks and praise, becomes so—for of course, abundance is everywhere. This practice of repeating these lines is so important because I have to unlearn fear and worry—and yet this gratitude is so pervasive, it seems eager to be learned. When I work to become aware of it, I see the beauty in a random flower, or the trusting eyes of an animal, or the laughter of a passing child, or a deep conversation with a friend. Abundance truly is a choice.

_____

What in my life sings out for thanks and praise?

13

What do you do with the secret verses of your heart? With your need for redemption, the story without words? With paradoxical truths, too private and nuanced to share, that cannot be printed or spoken aloud?

—Rev. Angela Herrera

"How's your prayer life?" one Unitarian Universalist minister asked me during an afternoon meeting where I was complaining about how hard it was to be newly sober. I was surprised she asked me that. How can you speak of prayer at a time like this? Can't you see how hard this is for me?

To be honest, my prayer life wasn't going too well. I was struggling to make time for it, because I was so busy distracting myself from the discomfort of new sobriety. When I felt like my skin was crawling, prayer was not the first option that came to mind.

And slowly, gently, over the course of time, it became easier to turn to prayer or meditation to find peace and comfort amidst difficult moments in my life. With continual practice, I began reaching for prayer rather than reaching for the food or the drugs or the alcohol. I eventually felt grateful for this question and the way it shook me up and out of myself, to bring my attention back to spiritual relationship.

How's my prayer life?

You're only given a little spark of madness.
You mustn't lose it.

—Robin Williams

There was a time when I believed that by getting sober I would lose the most creative parts of me. That it was through having a drink (or two or three) that I could laugh, or be funny, or show off, or have a good time.

It was only after I had achieved sustained sobriety and taken all the steps that were suggested that I realized that alcohol had been blocking me from the creativity I actually possessed. I found I could have fun, show off appropriately (but not make an ass of myself), and appreciate life and those around me.

I found that not only did I not lose my spark but I found who I really was when I wasn't always trying to cover it up.

———

Can I offer gratitude for that special spark of
madness that is in me?

15

*When our heart is in a holy place, when our
    heart is in a holy place,
We are blessed with love and amazing grace
When our heart is in a holy place.*

—JOYCE POLEY

Sometimes it feels as if gratitude is a sort of industry these days. Everyone wants you to buy into it, and sometimes when I am having One of Those Days I do not want to be one of the customers. I grow resentful of what seems like an easy or surface-level commitment. Or I feel lazy and don't want to think about moving my heart to any place, even if it is holy.

And yet, when I relax and let go of my need to control, when I am just present and mindful, when I am humble and can laugh a little at my rigidity, I can lean into gratitude. My kind of gratitude is deep, hard-won, a little sarcastic, and seasoned.

We seek the gratitude that is deeper than the simple "thanks." The kind that is not offhand or easy. We seek the gratitude that speaks to the hardest moments, the challenging hours, the chilling times, that which is hard-sought and found through wrestling with the truths of our lives. By embracing the difficulties with gratitude, we also embrace all that is difficult for each of us, and we affirm our whole selves—beautiful, imperfect blessings that we are.

---

*For what do I hold deep gratitude?
How is gratitude a practice in my life?*

The little things? The little moments?
They aren't little.

—JON KABAT-ZINN

Mindfulness is cultivated in the act of remaining present to whatever is before you—in the decision to do so. For those of us who struggle with addiction, and also for those of us who love people living with addiction, this can be hard. We have constantly kept our mind and our eye to the future, attempting to predict the next move, focusing on when we'll get our next fix or when our loved one may next use.

To remain present takes practice—it doesn't happen overnight. Yet each moment we are able to stay right here, in this moment, is a move toward cultivating mindfulness. Each moment we can notice what is going on with us without judgment and without thinking we should be somewhere else, doing something else, is a move toward bringing mindfulness into our days.

May we remain in the present moment. May we be curious rather than judgmental about our life circumstances. May we remain mindful and present to what is.

———————

What is going on around me right in this moment?

17

Smile, breathe, and go slowly.
—THICH NHAT HANH

One reason that I am committed to daily spiritual practice is to lessen my experience of anxiety. I believe that much of why I became mired in my addiction was to mask the feelings that accompany anxiety. Now I know that there are other, healthier ways of responding to these often difficult feelings. I don't have to drink, use medication (other than prescribed), or engage in unhealthy behavior to cover up my feelings.

Meetings of my Twelve-Step group are always helpful. I have never attended a meeting where I felt worse afterward. And in between, I can talk to others in recovery, or I can practice meditation, paying attention to what I am feeling in my body. I can pay attention to the moment, rather than wondering what might happen tomorrow.

I appreciate that Thich Nhat Hanh makes a simple three-item list for me: 1. Smile, which changes my brain chemistry. 2. Breathe, because sometimes focusing on my breathing gives me the calming pause I need, and other times, in my anxiety, I am literally holding my breath. And 3. Go slowly, knowing that everything doesn't have to be completed in this moment, even though my anxiety tells me otherwise.

Have I engaged in spiritual practice today?

May we go forth from this place thankful for the life
that sustains and renews us, and open to the grace
that surrounds and surprises us. May we go forth
from this place with openness and with thanksgiving!

—REV. CHARLES A. HOWE

What a great thing it is when I am able to remember that I do not have to face the challenges of life alone. For me, help and hope are found in religious community. Regular attendance and connection at my place of worship allow me to check in with myself and to see how I am doing week to week. I can take a moment every week to see how things are with my soul, and often, quite often, what I feel is gratitude.

I am grateful for community in my life in so many forms. Community nurtures me and keeps me going. One of the hard things about addiction is how its secrets keep you isolated—and isolation makes me feel as if I am not good enough for the company of others. By keeping company with others, I am able to remember my inherent goodness, the inherent wholeness that I only need to remember to restore. I am also better able now to assess which communities are good for my soul and which are not—and to know I am free to choose whether to participate in them or not.

———————

Where do I find a healing sense of community?
Where might I seek it further still?

19

It is always good to give thanks! All that we have is a gift from life: our food, our relationships, our shelter from the cold. And when we give thanks, it is always good to be mindful of all people, and notice those who are suffering and do what we can to ease suffering and change its causes.

—REV. MYKE JOHNSON

Living in addiction is a form of suffering. Each day brings a new opportunity to swear off the substance for good. And the cycle of addiction often brings us back to the substance again and again. It causes deep suffering of the mind, as we attempt to will into being a change that feels impossible. It causes deep suffering of the spirit, communicating to us that we have little worth and that if we were better people, we would not use. And it causes deep suffering of the body, as we take in poisonous substances that destroy our muscles, our brains, and many other parts of our bodies.

It is hard to feel grateful in the midst of such suffering.

And to get out of the cycle of addiction, we must first acknowledge that we are suffering. We must acknowledge that we can't keep doing this. We must face the truth of our mental, emotional, and spiritual suffering so we can then work with others and with a Higher Power to get free.

How have I experienced suffering?

Unless a practice cools the fires of greed, aversion, and ignorance it is worthless.

—JOSEPH GOLDSTEIN

I am not okay unless I have some daily form of spiritual practice in my life. While I used to be somewhat glib about what I considered a spiritual practice, I realize that I need to take spiritual practice seriously, which means that I do it regularly and with the intention of improving my quality of life.

I prepare and drink coffee daily, but it's not a spiritual practice, more of a meaningful ritual, because I find it a pleasant way to begin my day. But I have a friend who gets up, makes her coffee, and then sits with it while she does her spiritual reading. She does this without other distractions, and she does it daily. For her, this is a spiritual practice.

I meditate daily, at midday, and I have chosen this time intentionally as a good moment to recalibrate my day. I find that when I finish, I feel as if I have just received a jumbo dose of oxygen. I am ready to face what is next.

My meditation practice, my exercise practice, and my recovery practice all require focus, and I sometimes need to return to them when I've fallen off, but I take care to not be superficial about them, because they are an important part of my life.

———————

Does my practice cool the fires?

21

We are energized by the beauty of the day. May we make use of that energy to take part in the lifting of burdens. May our gratitude find expression in the care of others, both near and far. May we find ways to bless the world.

—REV. KERRY MUELLER

I have had to ponder whether gratitude is a choice. Having thought about it, I believe that it is. When I was living as a family member of those affected by addiction, I was not able to see that I had healthy choices. I was too busy trying to fix that which I could not fix and do what I could not do. I began to feel powerless and hopeless and as if I was a victim of circumstance. I began to feel as if I was the plaything of an all-powerful God I don't believe in—as if the only reality was some supernatural hostility toward me!

And then, little by little, I made different choices, and that made all the difference. How important it is to have a sense of faith that includes my own agency. Through hard work and focus, dedication, and sometimes just dogged determination to be consistent in caring for myself, I have come to see that I am a co-creator of my life and, as such, I have agency and worth and dignity. I can choose to be grateful and to be whole and to see my world through those lenses. I can choose the people to whom I entrust my vulnerable parts. I am grateful for my ability to heal and to set my own direction for that healing.

How do I choose to embrace my wholeness today?

*I am praying again
and how does one pray
when unsure if anything hears?*

    —Rev. Barbara Pescan

One of the teachers in my Twelve-Step recovery program tells us over and over again that Twelve-Step recovery is for anyone, atheists and agnostics included. The only requirement along the way is to believe in something greater and more important than yourself, which you can trust and rely upon. This teacher, who is an atheist, refers to virtues they hold high—love, beauty, truth, integrity—as parts of life that are larger than any one person's experience and upon which we can rely.

For some Unitarian Universalists, the concept of a Higher Power can be a barrier to getting into recovery. However you find it, whether in Twelve-Step fellowships or in other recovery programs, what is most important is that you find recovery. What is most important is that you get to live to see another day, that you do not die of this disease of addiction that has claimed countless lives.

Prayer can be so complicated for folks who identify as atheists and agnostics. Perhaps a place to start is a request for help or a simple "Thank you." Perhaps a place to start is next to a person in recovery who is also struggling. Perhaps a place to start is within our own hearts, considering the highest virtues we can and holding them in the esteem they deserve.

Which virtues in life do I hold high?

23

Many people . . . define spirituality as the search for meaning and purpose. But this is also a specific practice that can be learned, developed, and applied. It involves both seeking and making.

—FREDERIC AND MARY ANN BRUSSAT

Writers Frederic and Mary Ann Brussat continually encourage their readers to engage in spiritual practice. But sometimes the term seems so nebulous it's hard to know where to start.

In seeking meaning, it's good to step back, to look at the big picture that is your life and experience.

It's so easy to get caught up in the daily minutiae that I often forget to consider what it is that is my goal, or my aim, or my highest value. Seeking meaning invites me to consider that I can do this through prayer, or daily journaling, or a guided meditation.

Making meaning invites me to attach stories, or analogies, or symbols to things or events. Again, in order to do this, I must take time to consider which stories go with which events. I can do this in the same way and time I do the seeking. Having an end-of-the-day ritual helps me to make meaning.

———————

In what ways am I seeking and making meaning as a spiritual practice?

*May we be appreciative above all for the concern
and love of those around us; for the exceeding bliss
of the touch of the holy which suddenly awakens
our drowsy souls to the blessed awareness of the
divine within us and within others.*

24

—REV. MICHAEL LEDUC

We often speak of the seeds of gratitude, yet is gratitude the seed or the sower? Isn't gratitude the caster of those many small packages of hope that can be sprinkled throughout the ordinariness of our days? Those stirrings of possibility that can sprout in an area of our lives? Isn't gratitude the actor whose gifts invite us into a larger story of meaning in our lives? How do we greet the sower of gratitude—even if the hand that tosses the seeds is ours?

To the beauty in my life, I say yes.

To the hope seeded in my life, I offer thanks.

To the people who make life bearable and wonderful, I extend a hearty "amen!"

To the troubles that I would not wish and yet know I will survive, I give a nod. To life, oh yes, to life!

----

*What one specific thing can I do to sow the
seeds of gratitude in my life?*

25

*Once they realize that we are indeed their children,
that we are indeed everywhere, every myth, every lie,
every innuendo will be destroyed once and for all.*

—HARVEY MILK

Harvey Milk is one among many who inspire me to live authentically. As a member of the LGBTQ community, I have seen addiction ravage my life as well as the lives of those I love. We have lived with so much trauma in our lives—addiction and dysfunction in our families of origin, judgements from others about living our authentic lives.

When I was living with addiction, so much of my life became a secret; I was isolating all of the time. Those secrets ate away at me, where I felt simultaneously dependent upon them for my safety and resentful I had to keep parts of myself a secret from others.

Recovery has been such a gift, as I have learned more and more about telling my truth and turning that truth into a way to be of service to others. I have grown through living more openly and embracing the risks that come with working the steps in this program. Through that growth, I have been able to help others live a freer and more authentic life too.

---

*How can I live more boldly so that others may feel freer
to be themselves, too? How can I be brave in my living,
to provide a beacon to others struggling to get free?*

Give all to love;
Obey thy heart;
Friends, kindred, days,
Estate, good-fame,
Plans, credit and the Muse,—
Nothing refuse.

   —RALPH WALDO EMERSON

How does one listen to their heart?

The answer lies in consistent practice, intentional time, and honoring what one hears. It's not something we can just say we will do, and it happens. To listen to the heart is to sit in quiet, to honor the instincts and the intuition.

If we are living with addiction, perhaps the desire of our hearts has grown cloudy. There are times when our very being screams out for the fix, for the substance. And moments when all we want is to stop.

If we have loved someone struggling with addiction, perhaps the desire of our hearts has gotten wrapped up in our desire for the other person to recover. It is hard to listen to our own hearts when the lives of others are at stake.

Taking this intentional time for ourselves draws our attention back to the one place where we can make a difference: within ourselves. To listen to the heart and honor what we hear builds relationship with the spirit, with the heart, and with the self.

Where can I make time to listen to my heart's longings?

27

When you plant seeds in the garden, you don't dig them up every day to see if they have sprouted yet. . . . Abandon impatience and instead be content creating the causes for goodness; the results will come when they're ready.

—THUBTEN CHODRON

Kenneth Jones and Tema Okun include in their list of characteristics of white supremacy culture a constant sense of urgency and the idea that "progress" means things getting bigger and more numerous. These do not just undermine racial justice; they are also counterproductive to serenity. While it may be urgent to work toward creating justice and halting climate change, I can't do that work unless I have a sense of calm. Ways to counter these harmful characteristics include making realistic work plans that include quality goals.

I may see green leaves coming from the ground, but if I go ahead and yank on them right away, I'll get a handful of greens with no carrot attached. I have to wait, keep on watering, and wait some more. This might be obvious to someone who doesn't struggle with an addictive disposition, but I've got to keep reminding myself to settle down, to wait, to keep on practicing.

The beauty of continuing to practice, to wait, to do just one thing at a time is that through patience, I am gifted with not only carrots but also another day of sobriety.

Can I use the counters to white supremacy culture to add to my spiritual practice?

Be patient toward all that is unsolved in
your heart and to try to love the questions
themselves like locked rooms and like books
that are written in a very foreign tongue.

—RAINER MARIA RILKE

One of the consequences of living touched by addictions is that I can need to feel as if I have more answers than I do. I need to feel as if I am in more control than I am. I need to be right. All of these traits get in the way of the open-heartedness and the curiosity I need in order to move into a newer and healthier way of being.

I am trying to cultivate a tentative gratitude for the times I make a mistake and certain gratitude for the times I can allow myself to admit my mistakes, make amends, seek forgiveness, and move forward. The opportunity to be a learner is a gift—and if I am honest, I am and always will be a learner. I think that is true for all of us, especially me who needs to unlearn so much in order to thrive. Allowing myself to be a beginner in the face of new truths and an apprentice learning a healthier way of managing the world is essential to my survival. I cannot and do not do it right all the time, and the gift in that is that I can be grateful for that truth.

———————

How am I grateful for the opportunity to learn
and admit my mistakes?

29

There is a love holding me.
There is a love holding all that I love.
There is a love holding all.
I rest in this love.

—REV. REBECCA PARKER

As I seek through prayer and meditation to improve my conscious contact with that mysterious source of all existence, I find sung prayer, a kind of lectio divina, helpful.

Unitarian Universalist musician and composer Elizabeth Norton wrote a beautiful piece of music for Rebecca Parker's prayer of affirmation. When simple yet profound language is set to music, suddenly it becomes infinitely repeatable. When I am part of a group singing this song in a round, I am moved and truly feel held.

Spiritual practice is not only something that needs to be repeated but also something that can bring a deep sense of peace. When I sing a song affirming the love of which we are all part, I feel connected, a part of a community.

I have many more songs committed to memory than I realize. I can call them up at will, singing, for example, "Go now in peace, go now in peace; may the love of God surround you everywhere, everywhere you may go." And now I have a blessing to offer to my loved ones as we leave the house each day.

Can I learn a prayer today to create a singing meditation?

*The lens of gratitude allows us to know a truth as
precious as a single snowflake, to grasp a love as
expansive as a lifetime, to feel the miraculous as
steady as a pulse, to see the grain of wheat amidst
the chaff, to sense the pearl of potential in the oyster,
to see another as the ordinary magnificence, . . .
to find the joy that frees the spirit.*

—REV. LESLIE TAKAHASHI

I cannot be grateful for something that I am not aware of.
For this reason, mindfulness and gratitude are like friends,
journeying hand in hand. Awareness of the small beauties
and countless precious moments of life is an important
counterweight to the difficulty which I seem to drag with
me as the legacy of my experience with addiction. In order
to receive the healing medicines of gratitude, I have to
notice the world around me and I have to be grateful for
what I notice.

When I pay attention to the world, I am able to see its
wonders. When I don't, I can fall back into my old and tired
complaints and woes. I want to be in the company of the
perceptive friend, mindfulness, who helps guide me over to
the side of the generous friend, gratitude. In their company,
I can heal and restore myself to the wholeness that others
did not see, and yet which is my birthright.

———————

*How can I cultivate the mindfulness that is the
foundation of a daily practice of gratitude?*

December

Having had a spiritual awakening
as the result of these steps, we
sought to carry the message to
other addicts and to practice these
principles in all our affairs.

And let us consider how to provoke one another to love and good deeds, not neglecting to meet together, as is the habit of some, but encouraging one another, and all the more as you see the Day approaching.

—HEBREWS 10:24–25

After a career of walking along high steel beams, climbing in awkward, dangerous places, and crouching down in his welding hood, my husband retired early. Although sometimes he used to come home from fourteen-hour days crotchety, he long ago was given the moniker "the mayor," because he has a way of being friendly and engaged in the world around him.

In our neighborhood, children are always out and ready to explore their surroundings. My husband noticed a couple of boys investigating the areas around the nearby fields. A bit later, he saw them with bows and arrows, the kind used in target shooting. They were creeping up upon the feeding deer, using the animals as a target. He stopped and reminded them, with his attitude of love and care, that they'd need to eat whatever they killed. Were they prepared?

Those arrows, with their blunt tips, would only have bounced off the animals' sides if they even managed to hit them. But I love how he is willing to engage with the people around him, becoming a part of the community, and in so doing, building relationship.

Where might I engage with community?
How can I practice kindness?

Most of us, along the way, have learned the gift,
the wonder, the awe, the healing blessings of
nurturing. Giving and receiving is a continuous
cycle, a necessary part of the road to the heart.

—MELODY BEATTIE

I could never go as deep or get to the places I have gone
without the help of others. This is the Seventh Principle of
Unitarian Universalism: "Respect for the interdependent
web of all existence of which we are a part." For a time, I
could see the ways we were connected in the world. But
what was my part? How was I claiming that I was a part of
this interdependent web?

I felt I had no capacity to care for others. Through the
care and careful attention of others, I began a process of
healing, accompanied by folks in my program who also
struggled. Eventually I realized that, to honor the help and
encouragement I had been given, I needed to be helpful
to others.

Through offering that care, through being in conversation with the people around me, through offering to be
helpful, I got outside of myself and got to a deeper place of
recovery. To give away what had been given to me honored
the interdependence of human community and healing.

How am I claiming my role in the interdependent
web of existence of which we are all a part?

3

Everything has its beauty,
but not everyone sees it.

—Confucius

I recently put up a bird feeder outside of my office. It is cone-shaped, black with a yellow top, and has little slats from which the birds can eat. As I am sending an email or typing a report, I often find myself looking up at the feeder. More than once I have caught sight of a beautiful creature nibbling away, its red, blue, or yellow feathers flickering in the sunlight. The feeder has become a way of inviting beauty into my day.

Service can be a lot like that, too. When we find ways to be generous with others, we often find that beauty comes across our path. I remember sitting with my first sponsee as he went through his inventory. Like most of us, he revealed some tender parts of his life story. It turned into a very human moment of connection, both tender and vulnerable. It was beautiful. When we choose to serve others, we create the space for that sort of beauty to show up.

When has serving others or giving to others
opened a space for beauty in my life?

Each day, somewhere in the world, recovery begins when one alcoholic talks with another alcoholic, sharing experience, strength, and hope.

> —ALCOHOLICS ANONYMOUS,
> "THE BIG BOOK"

There's nothing quite like talking with someone who's been through something similar to what you are facing, especially when it comes to the disease of addiction. For someone brand new in recovery, talking with another person who has been addressing their problems even a little longer can be just the way to open up the mind and heart to finally acknowledge that life has become unmanageable.

For the person in recovery longer, sharing experience, strength, and hope is being of service. It is not only giving back; it also keeps recovery growing, helps develop spiritual maturity, and reminds both people that there is a solution to the old selfish and self-centered way of being.

Recovery is a long-term practice, and it can bring a joy in living that is ultimately satisfying. It starts when one addict talks with another, sharing their experience, the strength they have found, and the hope that another person can recover.

Can I find a meeting today where I can share my experience, strength, and hope?

5

Every day brings struggle, every day brings joy.
Every day brings us the opportunity to ease the
struggle of another, to be the joy in another's life.

—VANCE BASS

I have been guilty of the expectation that recovering from my addiction would make my life perfect. I would finally be happy, and all would work out. Turns out, life is not like that. Some days are great. Others are tough. More days have been better since I've been in recovery, and I would not trade my life now for the life I had before, any day.

There are times when new people attend meetings, or folks who are still struggling with addiction are in the rooms, and I am instantly reminded of where I have been. When I first began recovery, I wanted to distance myself from the folks who were struggling. They might disrupt the serenity I had worked so hard to achieve. They served as reminders of a place I never wanted to go back to.

And then I relapsed. And I found myself being that same person in recovery, desperately reaching out for help, going back to the place where all of my struggles were visible. In retrospect, this relapse was a beautiful reminder that I cannot believe I have this figured out and have nothing to learn from folks still struggling in the illness of addiction. There is often an opportunity to reach out and connect, to ease the struggle of another.

———————

Who is someone I can connect with today, to ease
their struggles or have my struggles eased?

Doing nothing for others is the undoing of ourselves.
—HORACE MANN

One of my favorite fantasy films is Neil Gaiman's *Coraline*. The movie's title character moves with her parents into a new home. Late one night, Coraline discovers a small door that leads to a tunnel. When she gets to the tunnel's other end, she discovers a strange new world. This world is much like her old one—it has the same house, same family, and same friends. The major difference is that everyone in this world is there to make Coraline happy. Her new mom gives her everything that she wants, and her new dad seems to exist for the sole purpose of entertaining her. Coraline never has to do anything unless it is easy and enjoyable.

The new world doesn't work out so well. It turns out that a world that is designed to only make you happy should come with a warning label. I think that's because we need opportunities to serve, to be generous, to give. Without those things, the world of our dreams looks a little too much like a nightmare. In a way, the journey Coraline takes to get home again is a lot like the journey to sobriety: we go from an isolated world that is all about us to a world where we are given the opportunity to care about others.

How might moving toward community provide meaning that I might otherwise be lacking?

Success doesn't motivate me as much as integrity does. Everyone loses. I enjoy the pressure of showing up every single day, being focused, putting forth my best effort, getting the best out of my teammates, and enjoying the journey.

—BECKY SAUERBRUNN

I stopped procrastinating and finally asked someone to be my new sponsor. We had known each other for quite a while, and she knew I had worked with other sponsors over the years. But she asked me to make it a priority to attend the particular meeting that she attended. I had attended in the past, but the meeting was just a handful of women who were really struggling. Not my people. I sighed and rolled my eyes. "Why do I need to go to this meeting?"

"This meeting needs help," she calmly replied.

And I knew that if I wanted her to work with me, I needed to do as she asked. So I showed up. Week after week on that Monday night. At first I knew that I needed to listen and to share my story. To keep coming back, so that that meeting had a few women who had some experience that could give hope to these people who were brand new, still in a fog.

Week after week I came, and began to enjoy the journey, and, as the group grew larger and larger, I made friends, became a sponsor myself, and grew to love that thriving group of women.

How might my showing up every single day be an act of integrity?

I have been so consumed with my own hurts that I've forgotten to call a friend whose hurt is equal to my own. I put off doing those things that might bring healing to someone who is broken, or joy to someone who is sad, or compassion to someone who is at odds with the rhythm of life, because I cared more for my own loneliness.

—Rev. Elizabeth Tarbox

When I first entered a recovery program, I believed I was only there for my own healing. I thought I would get what I needed and get out. It's a common story, all about me getting sober and getting my needs met.

Unexpectedly, as my recovery journey progressed, so many people reached out to get to know me and to offer help. When I think of the time my sponsor has spent with me over the phone or in person, offering kind words and uncomfortable reminders, it can bring me to tears. This is a program where people are ready to give.

What I eventually learned was that in reaching out to others who were struggling or new, I was able to get out of my own head and into helping others. This is my Unitarian Universalist values at their best. We do good works because we know our spiritual health depends upon it. I am so grateful to have grown beyond the story of getting what I needed and getting out.

Is there someone I can reach out to help,
right now or sometime today?

9

Children betrayed their parents by becoming their own people.

—LESLYE WALTON

Of all the religious holidays, I especially love the ones at this time of year. But along with the beauty of the darkness and twinkling lights come unrealistic expectations that peace will prevail or even somehow, this year, we'll all get along better.

Before my relatives arrive, I am excitedly anticipating the joy we'll share and the things we'll give each other: not just Christmas presents, but also time spent talking and playing games together, expressions of love and support, and long, elaborate shared meals. But these are things that I want, not necessarily what others want or need.

Then there's the fact that the square footage that works for my partner and me is suddenly going to have to be enough for six of us. It might have worked when the kids were young, but now they're full-grown adults who can't all fit on the loveseat.

The message of generosity and giving, repeated at church and throughout the community at this season, might need extra emphasis at home. It means that I can be more generous of spirit, not expecting everything to go my way, and I can be more tolerant of annoyances, especially when we're crammed in all together.

How might I offer my family a more expansive generosity?

Wonder trumps anxiety. We cannot be filled with wonder and remain anxious at the same time. Wonder is the ability to feel amazement, admiration and curiosity about something. Wonder invites our best, most creative thinking. Wonder connects us with God. So how do we move from anxiety to wonder?

—SUSAN BEAUMONT

Susan Beaumont points out that anxiety can cripple both institutions and individuals. She writes, "The voices of judgment, cynicism and fear run amok in anxious times. They cultivate a closed mind, heart and spirit. They fight against wonder. If our desire is to adopt a non-anxious leadership stance then we need to release these voices."

I love wonder, but often find myself filled with anxiety. In recent years I learned to take more time with the elements of recovery, especially when I'm the busiest, to counteract the incapacitating results of anxiety. Over the years since I have been practicing these principles, I have come to see that anxiety was the main contributor to my addiction.

In this season that brings us many stressful holidays, I want to remember that wonder trumps anxiety. I want to offer wonder to the world and to my own heart.

How can I bring my best non-anxious self to the groups that I participate in?

Let our lives be a prayer
That waters dry souls
Mends broken hearts
Refuses to be terrorized
Seeks this world's beauty
And carries us through its storms.

—REV. JOEL MILLER

Step Twelve invites each of us "to practice these principles in all our affairs." When they wrote them, the authors of these Steps were speaking to the principles of the recovery program. As a Unitarian Universalist, I wonder about practicing our Seven Principles in all of my affairs.

This Step invites me to welcome the UU Principles into my daily interactions. How can I honor the inherent worth and dignity of the person who just cut me off in traffic? Can I affirm another person's free and responsible search for truth and meaning when they aren't doing what I want them to do? Can I say I am committed to justice, equity, and compassion in human relations when I benefit from the forced labor of incarcerated people without working against the system that exploits them?

Step Twelve is a gift. A time to check in on how we are living the principles of recovery and our faith in our daily lives. It gives us space to take stock, acknowledge where we have fallen short, and aspire once again to live by the guiding principles written on our hearts.

Where can I see one of my guiding principles alive
in my life today?

*Now notice your feet on the floor. Feel your connection
to this meetinghouse and its old stone foundation
grounded in the earth, connecting us to the
generations who have gathered here before us.
Ancestors whose presence lingers in this sacred space.
What dreams and visions did they pursue here?*

—REV. ISRAEL BUFFARDI

Asking for help from others is hard. The first time I met someone who identified as a compulsive overeater, it took me a year to get up the courage to ask them to help me, to talk with me about their experience. When I did, I felt like a burden, like I was asking something intrusive, like they would never want to talk to me because their addiction was a secret too.

But they met with me and offered so much help and experience. I felt less alone. I felt understood in a way I had not felt before. At the end of our time together I thanked them, and their response was "Someone else shared with me, and now I'm sharing with you."

All of us need help. And the help we are receiving is often from other people who have been helped by someone else. It's a deep reminder of the Seventh Principle of Unitarian Universalism, respect for the interdependent web of all existence of which we are a part. I have been helped because someone else helped someone. It's a never-ending chain of interdependent mutuality.

––––––––––

*Who has helped me in the recent past?
Who have I offered help to?*

13

The heart that gives, gathers.
—Marianne Moore

The Palestinian-American poet Naomi Shihab Nye says that happiness is a thing that comes and goes at will, leaping from one rooftop to the next, and that by the time it lands on your home it is already preparing to leave. In other words, we can't control it. It arrives when it arrives, and it leaves when it leaves. It is not something that can be kept for good, and it is certainly not something that can be bought.

When I traveled to New Orleans to do service work after Hurricane Katrina, I discovered a world with not much happiness left in it. The storm had taken everything, or at least most things. But what I discovered in that context is that the happiness that could be found was in small acts of kindness and generosity. It was in service to others. So much else—diplomas, achievements, things that you buy—meant so very little, while giving meant so very much.

I still remember the giant bear hug that one woman gave me after I had helped retrieve her family memorabilia from a home that had been torn apart. In that act of service, I felt a sort of happiness I had not experienced before, raw and unfiltered, jumping for just a moment onto my rooftop and lingering. What I found was that, in giving, I was receiving a happiness I had not anticipated.

Have I allowed myself recently to experience the joy of giving to others?

When I first got sober, I thought, my life is over.
My fun is done, and I'm not going to be cool anymore.
—ROB LOWE

Rob Lowe tells a story in his memoir about how connection with and the support of (cool) people helped keep him sober. After he came home from a rehab facility, he was contacted by people he didn't even know, urging him on in his recovery.

Now sober for over thirty years, Lowe has said in an interview, "I was so excited that I could still be cool and not have to be the life of the party."

I can't imagine what it would be like to be famous and have my mistakes published in magazines and on the Internet. Ordinary people may not get a phone call from celebrities, but one of the reasons for attending recovery meetings of any kind is for support. And once recovery has become a way of life, being of service to others keeps us sober and lets us give back something of what we have received.

———————

How might I be of service to someone today?

15

*Hold me accountable so I may bring honor to you,
amplify love and compassion to those around me,
and make the way easier for those yet to come.*

—Rev. Tandi Rogers

Making the way easier for those yet to come may not be our first thought when getting into recovery. But, at a certain point, we have wisdom to share with others, ways we can be helpful, and experiences that are probably shared.

We make the way easier for those yet to come by remaining available to people who are new, recognizing that we were new at this recovery thing at one point too. We make it easier by reaching out to people we know are struggling, offering to be helpful, but never proselytizing about what others should do. We make it easier by remembering all those who were willing to pick up the phone or sit with us or listen to us or offer their experience, having gone through similar things.

Doing this honors the many who have gone before us, and our actions ensure that others will find recovery programs available when they are in need.

How can I make the way easier for someone else?

The most important thing is to try and inspire people so that they can be great in whatever they want to do.
—KOBE BRYANT

In 1965, the AA convention held in Toronto adopted a statement that said, "I am Responsible. When anyone, anywhere, reaches out for help, I want the hand of A.A. always to be there. And for that: I am responsible."

That statement has been reaffirmed and printed on wallet cards, it is posted on the walls of rooms where meetings take place, and it has been used as a closing affirmation. It is a reminder to me to live with a sense of gratitude and appreciation. The book of Luke says that much will be required from those to whom much has been given, and my Unitarian Universalist religious tradition emphasizes "deeds, not creeds."

I believe the best way to live well is to be generous in spirit and in action. It brings joy, it makes a life fulfilled, and it keeps those with a predilection toward addiction firmly in recovery rather than focused on themselves.

There are so many ways to be of service, to give to others. I like helping people understand that religion, including my own Unitarian Universalist tradition, can embrace a liberal way of understanding and engaging with the world. I also believe it is my responsibility to help people who are looking for help getting sober. So I need to be engaged and show up. I can't leave it to someone else, just hoping they will do it.

How am I responsible when someone reaches out for help?

*In the authentic and gentle manner of our
    connections,
we cultivate a simple sweetness to brighten our
    spirits.
May we be grateful for the ways we nourish and
    uplift each other,
For it is the sharing of this hallowed time together
    that sustains us.*

—KATIE GELFAND

Authentic connections and relationships are such a gift. When two or more people can come together to join in relationship, not thinking about what one can get from the other, not thinking about how to manipulate others to get one's own needs met, this is such a gift.

Authenticity knows authenticity. We can see it in one another when the harsh armor of ego and image management falls away and the tenderness behind it all is revealed.

We need one another. And we are in need of relationships that are real—people we can be honest with, folks we can listen to and know they are telling the truth of their experience. Each time we come together in this way, the ground underneath us is sacred ground.

———————

Who can I be authentic with?

*Recovery is something that you have to work
on every single day and it's something that
doesn't get a day off.*

—DEMI LOVATO

The slogan "one day at a time" is popular in recovery circles, and it has become a favorite in popular culture as well, given the stress levels of people's lives. It has a Buddhist bent to it, reminding us to stay in the moment, not to get caught up in worry about things that haven't happened yet.

I don't like to think of recovery like exercise, where if you don't work on that muscle you lose it, but when I remember to stay in the moment, I am actually working on my recovery. It's good for me to engage in the healthy tools I have learned, like prayer, like reading some kind of recovery material, like attending a meeting, like reaching out to another person who is in recovery, like doing some reflection on my day ahead and, at the end of the day, the twenty-four hours just behind me.

When I can remember to pay attention to my serenity and recovery each day, my life is better. I can live my life in gratitude.

---

*Just for today, what can I do to focus
on my recovery?*

19

In the end it won't matter how much we have,
but how generously we have given.
It won't matter how much we know,
but rather how well we live.

—Rev. John C. Morgan

As a child growing up in an alcoholic home, I was raised with a sense of scarcity. Because my alcoholic parent was constantly and frivolously spending money, it felt like the rest of us had to save or do without. To be generous didn't really feel like an option. To give felt like a luxury reserved for people who had means beyond our own.

I took this learning into adulthood and remained in a fearful mindset of scarcity, never believing I had enough time or money or love or resources to meet my own needs. I hoarded these all to myself, believing that they would fill the emptiness I felt inside. It was hard to see beyond my own circumstances.

As I recover from the effects of growing up in an alcoholic home, I am unlearning this mindset of scarcity, recognizing when this old fear rears its head. There is most certainly enough to go around. To be generous is a part of acknowledging that there are enough love and money and time and resources to live a life of purpose and meaning.

Where is one place that I can be generous today?

*I have found that among its other benefits,
giving liberates the soul of the giver.*

— MAYA ANGELOU

Nicholas Kristof wrote that there are three basic pleasures that human beings crave: food, sex, and giving. That last one is not something that we hear about very much. Few people mention that giving is an intrinsic human need. In fact, the statement flies in the face of the popular idea that human beings are hardwired to look out for number one.

Kristof argues that this is wrong. Deep down, people want to give. They desire the meaning that comes with giving. According to brain scans, they crave it as much as they crave food and sex. I once heard a minister say that in his decades of church work no one ever said to him, "I really wish you would tell me how to be more selfish." No one ever knocked on the door to his office and complained, "Why don't you tell me about how meaning is for the birds, and cash and prizes are all that matter?"

That's probably why millions of people volunteer, donate money, give blood, and show up for one another in times of need. They make time to give themselves away, so they can give their lives meaning and purpose. That practice is so different from addiction, which produces only an empty and selfish pleasure. In giving and in service, we find a pleasure that is purer, more sustaining, and fundamentally lifegiving.

How might I find a new way to be of service to others?

21

The best way to not feel hopeless is to get up and do something. Don't wait for good things to happen to you. If you go out and make some good things happen, you will fill the world with hope, you will fill yourself with hope.

—BARACK OBAMA

What a beautiful gift to keep us active in recovery! I can be of service, be of use, I can go out into the world to make it better. Whenever I choose to begin my day this way, even when things go wrong, I am on a positive track. I'm not self-absorbed or caught up in the difficulties that seem to face me.

It's like the parable of the starfish thrower. It is told in many ways, but here's one you may like: I was walking on the beach one morning and saw another person, who looked amazingly like me, throwing starfish after starfish into the water. Still, hundreds remained stranded on the sand, washed up and suffocating.

"Why do you keep throwing those starfish back? What difference can you make?"

The thrower responded, while tossing another joyfully back, "I made a difference to that one."

———————

What difference can I make today?

They come in ritual procession, these gifts of life.
Whether we deserve them we cannot know or say,
For they are poured out for us.
Our task is to hold steady the chalice of our being.

—Rev. Richard S. Gilbert

Pay attention to those who come bearing gifts.

It may not be someone you expect a gift from, a family member or a spouse or a close friend. It may be the person who created the chair you sit upon, the nameless individual who grew the vegetables you prepared for your dinner, the dear soul whose labor made a part of your day possible.

Pay attention to those who come bearing gifts.

Unexpected gifts. Gifts we certainly did not earn and cannot deserve. Gifts in the form of a helpful word or a listening ear. Gifts from God and gifts from human hands. Gifts of time to yourself and time spent with those who nourish your spirit. Gifts that give you life.

Pay attention to those who come bearing gifts.

And meet those gifts with gratitude and appreciation. For these gifts make up the days of our living. They are the lifeblood that sustains us.

Who has come into my life bearing gifts today?

Attention is the rarest and purest form of generosity.
—SIMONE WEIL

John Gottman is a therapist who has interviewed thousands of couples in order to see what makes their relationships work. He claims that he can usually tell in the first fifteen minutes whether a relationship is likely to last or dissolve. He has developed seven principles of relationships that he tries to instill in the people he works with.

One of Gottman's principles is turning toward each other. In his book he gives the example of a wife who is looking out the window, and says something bland to her husband, such as "I wonder if the neighbors are moving," or "It looks like spring is here." On the surface, it sounds meaningless, more like an observation than a question that would require a response. But Gottman says that these frivolous statements often constitute a bid for connection. They are subtle attempts to be seen by one's partner. If one's partner never responds to such statements, the foundation of the relationship can begin to corrode.

Before I was in recovery, I did not pay very much attention to the needs of other people. Now that I have the clarity of sobriety, I find that I can more readily bring this attention to my interactions. In ways small and large, I can help the ones I love feel both seen and heard.

How might I make someone feel seen, heard,
or appreciated today?

There's no shame in enjoying a quiet life. And that's been the realization of the past few years for me.

—DANIEL RADCLIFFE

I've heard expressions of actual fear from those who are making the decision to take drinking out of their lives, a fear that they are giving up fun. Now, they are afraid, they'll not have fun anymore.

Yet the "big book" of Alcoholics Anonymous says with assurance, "We are not a glum lot."

Rather than having "fun" at night and lots of regret the next morning, now I can enjoy myself without a sense of impending doom.

Introverts, who have been pushing themselves to be the life of the party, can realize that life is good without needing to be the center of attention. Parties aren't the only things that can bring a sense of community.

I can now make decisions about how to spend my time with a sense of gratitude rather than a feeling of compulsion. I have found joy and peace in being of service, and I have found cheer in sobriety.

Where can I find conviviality today without engaging in unhealthy behavior?

25

No one has ever become poor by giving.
— ANNE FRANK

It's amazing to me how much the Twelve-Step concepts support each other. I have been particularly impressed recently with the ways that acceptance and service are related. When I was first learning to accept the reality of my addiction, I found that service was key. "Show up and make coffee" was one of the suggestions that my first sponsor made when I was just starting. And indeed, serving others made a big difference. It helped me stay grounded and get connected.

It was only later that I realized the opposite is also true: acceptance has an important place in service work. Specifically, it is important to accept things as they are and not be attached to outcomes and expectations. This is because not every person who you try to assist is going to receive your help. Not every person whom you offer advice to is going to take it. Not every gift that you have to offer will be welcomed by the receiver.

The lesson I take is this: Acceptance of one's addiction without serving others is unsustainable; service without accepting things for what they are can quickly lead to efforts to control and disappointment. But when we see the two as linked, a new way of living opens before us.

What am I trying to control that I might let go of?
How has acceptance contributed to my
spiritual growth?

You are what you do, not what you say you'll do.
—CARL GUSTAV JUNG

There's a story that a friend once went to visit Niels Bohr, the Nobel Prize–winning physicist, and saw a horseshoe hanging over his door. "Surely you don't believe that a horseshoe brings good luck!" exclaimed the friend incredulously. "Oh, no," Bohr replied, "but I heard that it works whether you believe in it or not."

I have come to think of service in this way. There are times when I do not feel like engaging in service. There are days when I do not believe that reaching out to others or showing up for a meeting will do much good. But there have been many, many times when, in spite of my misgivings, showing up for service has worked. Helping has got me out of my own cares and worries and has made a difference to others, whether I believed it would or not.

So no, I don't know whether horseshoes actually bring good luck. But I have learned that the tools of sobriety work whether you believe in them or not. You just have to make a point of using them.

---

*What has been holding me back from
being of service today?*

27

No one is useless in this world who lightens the burden of another.

—CHARLES DICKENS

This year my Unitarian Universalist congregation sponsored an Easter egg and canned food hunt for the neighborhood. A few of the older youth who arrived early were asked to help with the hiding. One of the younger children who happened to catch a glimpse of the older youth doing this walked up to me and asked, "Why is it that we need to help the Easter Bunny hide his eggs?"

"Well," I stumbled, trying to think on my feet, "sometimes the Easter Bunny is really busy and we get to be his helpers." The young boy seemed satisfied and rushed off to the sanctuary.

Even though I uttered that response without a whole lot of time to think about it, I believe there is some truth in it. We can't necessarily depend on someone else—Easter Bunny or human being—to do the good that needs to be done. By working a program, we are given countless opportunities to do good and to be of help in the world.

———————

How have I been able to provide help to another person, perhaps in an unexpected way?

Do not neglect to show hospitality to strangers,
for thereby some have entertained angels unawares.
—Hebrews 13:2

The process of recovery has been one of slowly allowing strangers to become friends to become trusted confidantes.

When I first entered the rooms of recovery, I thought I had nothing in common with the people around me. Turns out that is a very common story. So many of us come in with preconceived notions of who seeks recovery. These prejudgments sometimes keep us from getting the help that we need.

As I kept listening, I kept hearing my truth and my story being told by others. I realized so many of us have common experiences. And how couldn't we? None of us in that room was terminally unique. We all struggled either with loving others who lived with an addiction or with the symptoms and effects of our own addiction.

These strangers who I sat with slowly became friends. People I could call on when I needed help. Folks I could be honest with because they knew where I was coming from. As my recovery progressed, they became people who I would call in the midst of my struggles: people to be honest with, to pray with, and to ask for guidance in how to cope with what I was telling them about. These strangers are no longer strangers. They are me and I am them.

Where do I have an opportunity to get closer to
someone I think of as a stranger?

29

The purpose of life is not to be happy. It is to be useful, to be honorable, to be compassionate, to have it make some difference that you have lived and lived well.

—Ralph Waldo Emerson

I have found that sobriety is intimately linked with serving others. If I am isolated, I know I am moving away from growth. But when I am able to give and to exercise compassion in my relationships with others, I know that I am getting a little bit further along on my spiritual path.

In moments when I hear about the world's suffering and do not respond with compassion, I know I am going into isolation mode. Children being separated from their parents, incidents of police brutality, stories of folks who are starving and not provided for—these are moments to lean into being of service to others and not to numb my heart to the suffering all around me. The world is made a better place by the active participation of all to meet the needs for safety and security for all.

To remain sober, I must remain helpful. To remain truly helpful, I must keep a soft, open, and compassionate heart. To remain compassionate is to grow beyond what I had previously thought possible. It is creating the world we want to live in one relationship, one human interaction at a time.

How has my spiritual growth been connected with compassion and service?

I cannot do all the good that the world needs.
But the world needs all the good that I can do.

—JANA STANFIELD

The news covers a lot of terrible things, including disasters that are both natural and human made. Sometimes the news also includes stories about those who step in to help. Often those stories are about grand, heroic gestures. Someone rescues a person from a burning building, or sends millions of dollars for assistance, or intervenes to stop an act of violence.

I have always liked hearing those news stories. They are uplifting and admirable. But what I have been coming to appreciate more recently are the smaller acts of service and generosity that make a difference in people's lives. They are everyday acts and so don't get a lot of attention. But they can nonetheless make a huge difference to people. Showing up at a funeral. Calling a newcomer at a meeting. Offering to rake leaves for an elderly neighbor.

Part of this appreciation is linked with humility, I think. The smaller, humbler act of service is likely to go unnoticed by most people. It will certainly not make the news. But such acts are nonetheless essential. The idea of a world bereft of them is not pleasant, but a life filled with lots of them just might turn out to be meaningful.

What small act of service or generosity
might I provide today?

31

You cannot do a kindness too soon because you never know how soon it will be too late.

—RALPH WALDO EMERSON

Generosity and kindness are strength giving. Scientists once conducted a study that demonstrates this. They took one person at a time into a small room. They asked that person to hold out her arm. For about two minutes, she was berated and belittled. The researcher then tried to push her arm toward the floor and found almost no resistance.

She was then sent into another room with another researcher. The same experiment was repeated, only this time she was told many kind things about herself. When the researcher tried to push her arm to the floor this time, she was easily able to resist.

We may think that our small acts of service do not amount to much, but often they have effects on others that we cannot see. They can be the very things that strengthen people and make them better able to meet the challenges in their lives.

To maintain our sobriety, we must work with others in a way that builds them up. When we are generous with one another, we are ready to face whatever obstacles might come our way to challenge our sobriety. We are better together than we are alone.

———————

Has anyone recently done an act of generosity or kindness that made a difference for me? How might I be of service today?

RESOURCES

Recovery Programs

Alcoholics Anonymous   **aa.org**
Narcotics Anonymous   **na.org**
Overeaters Anonymous   **oa.org**
Al-Anon   **al-anon.org**
Adult Children of Alcoholics   **adultchildren.org**

Unitarian Universalist Resources

UU Addictions Ministry   **uuaddictionsministry.org**

Twelve-Step Unitarian Universalists: Essays on Recovery, edited by Ken and Cathlean

The Addiction Ministry Handbook: A Guide for Faith Communities, by Denis Meacham

"Twelve Steps, Seven Principles: UUs in Alcoholics Anonymous," by Michelle Huneven, archive.uuworld.org/2000/0100feat1.html